"If you've ever wished for snazzier words to clothe your thoughts, *Smart Words* is a bottomless wardrobe of elegant and sophisticated options."

—**Erin McKean, editor of** ***VERBATIM: The Language Quarterly***

"*Smart Words* is the perfect 'elbow book'—one that you will always want to have nearby as you are looking for the perfect words to make your point. Mim Harrison puts powerful, evocative words in your vocabulary as she asks her reader: why merely criticize when you can *castigate*, or why be indirect when you can be *circuitous*?"

—**Paul Dickson,** author of *The Dickson Baseball Dictionary, Third Edition*, and *Family Words: A Dictionary of the Secret Language of Families*

"Word learners and word lovers will find *Smart Words* a cornucopia of fascinating yet useful words. The chatty and clever clues to each word's meaning, and the lively, inventive, and offbeat sample sentences showing the words in context will keep you turning the pages to learn more. Grow your vocabulary here and have fun doing it."

—**Robert Greenman,** former journalism teacher and author of *Words That Make a Difference*

Smart Words

vocabulary for the Erudite*

*and those who wish to be

Mim Harrison

A PERIGEE BOOK
A STONESONG PRESS BOOK

A PERIGEE BOOK
Published by the Penguin Group
Penguin Group (USA) Inc.
375 Hudson Street, New York, New York 10014, USA
Penguin Group (Canada), 90 Eglinton Avenue East, Suite 700, Toronto, Ontario M4P 2Y3, Canada
(a division of Pearson Penguin Canada Inc.) • Penguin Books Ltd., 80 Strand, London WC2R 0RL,
England • Penguin Group Ireland, 25 St. Stephen's Green, Dublin 2, Ireland (a division of Penguin
Books Ltd.) • Penguin Group (Australia), 250 Camberwell Road, Camberwell, Victoria 3124,
Australia (a division of Pearson Australia Group Pty. Ltd.) • Penguin Books India Pvt. Ltd., 11
Community Centre, Panchsheel Park, New Delhi—110 017, India • Penguin Group (NZ), 67
Apollo Drive, Rosedale, North Shore 0632, New Zealand (a division of Pearson New Zealand Ltd.)
• Penguin Books (South Africa) (Pty.) Ltd., 24 Sturdee Avenue, Rosebank, Johannesburg 2196,
South Africa

Penguin Books Ltd., Registered Offices: 80 Strand, London WC2R 0RL, England

While the author has made every effort to provide accurate telephone numbers and Internet
addresses at the time of publication, neither the publisher nor the author assumes any responsibility
for errors, or for changes that occur after publication. Further, the publisher does not have any
control over and does not assume any responsibility for author or third-party websites or their
content.

SMART WORDS
A Stonesong Press Book

Copyright © 2008 by Mim Harrison and the Stonesong Press, LLC
"Blurb" from *Burgess Unabridged: A Classic Dictionary of Words You Have Always Needed*
reprinted by permission of Walker Publishing Company. Copyright © 1914 by Gelett Burgess.
"Caboodle" reprinted by permission of International Creative Management, Inc. Copyright © 1935
by E. B. White.
Cover art and design by Liz Sheehan
Text design by Richard Oriolo

First edition: November 2008

Library of Congress Cataloging-in-Publication Data

Harrison, Mim.
    Smart words : vocabulary for the erudite, and those who wish to be / Mim Harrison.— 1st ed.
        p.   cm.
    "A Perigee Book." "A Stonesong Press Book."
    Includes bibliographical references and index.
    ISBN 978-0-399-53464-5 (pbk.)
    1. Vocabulary.   I. Title.
    PE1449.H265   2008
    428.1—dc22   2008028924

PRINTED IN THE UNITED STATES OF AMERICA

10 9 8 7 6 5 4 3 2 1

Most Perigee books are available at special quantity discounts for bulk purchases for sales
promotions, premiums, fund-raising, or educational use. Special books, or book excerpts, can also
be created to fit specific needs. For details, write: Special Markets, Penguin Group (USA) Inc., 375
Hudson Street, New York, New York 10014.

To my mother,

who has always been smart about words

Contents

Contents

Introduction

Whoever said sounding smart had to be painful?

This book is designed to get you on friendly terms with some of the smart words in our rich, diverse, ever-adaptable, and always surprising language, and to help you recall them in ways that might bring a smile or a spark.

Okay, so you won't go around saying *huzzah* every time your team scores. But what a great word to call up when you have to write something on those group-congratulations cards. And maybe you've been told that Latin is a dead language, but how can it be anything but alive and kicking when you can toss words like *quotidian* into daily conversation?

You'll find words that make you adept at saying the plain in fancy terms (*verisimilitude*) and the fancy in plain terms (*eke*), thanks to the grand collision in English between the Norman and Saxon tongues. And words that show how agile English is at shifting meanings (check out *maneuver*) and giving old words like *avatar* a second life.

Some words are here because of their interesting histories (*chivalry*, *oysterwench*), and a few for the way that memorable people in history have used them (Dylan Thomas with *bombilating*, Winston Churchill with *audacity*, E. B. White with *caboodle*).

You may find words you sort of knew the meaning of and that you'll now definitely know the meaning of (*sojourn* was one for me). Plus a few you might have sworn were related but aren't (there is no *snark* in *snarky*). And some that have perhaps been only a vague blip on your radar screen, but may now work even on a text-messaging screen (try *pelf*).

Smart Words will help you be smart about the words you use and the way you use them. Certain occasions call for the zinger verb, other occasions for the killer adjective, still others for the one-syllable wonder or the lofty literary allusion.

How smart of you to use these words like you own them. Because now, you do.

Fast Phonetics

For the most part, you should find the phonetics intuitive—there are none of those upside-down and inverted *e*'s (the improbably named *schwa*: ə).

The syllable to stress is the one in CAPITAL LETTERS. Here's the key for the vowels:

a	mat
ā	ate
ah	are
aw	yawn
e	end
ee	beet
i	in
ī	ice
o	hot
ō	home
oo	hoot
u	hum
ur	hurt
yoo	cute

1

Action!

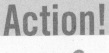

Keep the momentum going
with these vigorous verbs

We unleash the power of the language when we use the active voice. A ready supply of the right verbs to deploy helps you deliver sentences with a punch.

abscond to steal away (ab-SKOND)
> Those who steal must often steal away quickly and secretly—or abscond—from the scene of the crime.

He absconded so quickly that no one realized he was gone, and the jewels with him.

accrue to add or increase (uh-KREW)
> The word grows on you the more you use it; its root is in the Latin for "to grow."

Money accrues interest in a savings account.

burgeon to grow (BUR-jin)
> *Burgeon* is an outgrowth of the Old French word for "bud," and budding is what flowers and other growing things are so good at.

*Every year she planted more flowers, until her
backyard burgeoned into one of the most bountiful
gardens in the neighborhood.*

castigate to criticize severely (KASS-ti-gāt)
There's mean and then there's nasty. There's
criticize and then there's *castigate*. It doesn't get
much meaner or nastier.
*Why castigate someone for a minor infraction? Such
verbal punishment doesn't fit the purported crime.*

collude to conspire (kuh-LOOD)
Conspiracy theorists give this term lots of air
time, although just between us, we think they're
colluding against it.
*Lawmakers who meet in secret run the risk of
appearing to collude on a matter.*

confute to disprove (kun-FYOOT)
Rhymes with *refute*, which is another way to say it.
*Copernicus confuted the idea that the sun revolved
round the earth.*

coruscate to sparkle (KOR-us-kāt)
Flash this word around (*flash* is its root) when
you want to add a bit of gleam and glitter to the
conversation.
*The best diamonds and conversations have
something in common: they both coruscate.*

demonize to characterize as evil (DEE-mun-īz)
Of all the diabolical, devilish things to do to

4

someone (or something), demonizing is one of the worst.

Reformed smokers have been known to demonize the habit they finally kicked.

deracinate to uproot (di-RASS-i-nāt)

Don't get attached to this word. It's likely to pull up its roots anytime.

People who relocate frequently can feel deracinated, always pulling up stakes and never putting down roots.

disabuse to set a misconception straight (diss-uh-BYOOZ)

Own this word so that at least once in your life you can haughtily say, "Let me disabuse you of that notion."

You told me that climbing a mountain in a blizzard with a fifty-pound backpack would be exhilarating. Let me disabuse you of that notion.

dragoon to force (druh-GOON)

There's a dragon in the history of *dragoon*, which gives you an idea of just how fierce this coercion is.

The prisoners were dragooned into signing false confessions.

encumber to hinder (en-KUM-bur)

"Outta my way" is what you're tempted to say to those people and things that encumber. *Encumber* sets up a barrier and blocks the way.

The cummerbund was too tight around his waist and encumbered his movements.

enjoin to command or order (en-JOYN)

A word for every micromanager and bossy boss in the land—although the rest of us enjoin you not to do what this word says.

He barked orders all day, enjoining his staff to do the impossible.

evince to show clearly (ee-VINSS)

You can't be any clearer, as *evince* will convince that its meaning is evident.

Her broad grin evinced the happiness she felt.

eviscerate to remove something vital (i-VISS-uh-rāt)

This word is gutsy, and we mean that literally. In its raw sense, *eviscerate* means to pull out an internal organ, known as viscera.

Constant criticism can eventually eviscerate all sense of confidence.

exacerbate to aggravate (egg-ZASS-ur-bāt)

It's never good news with this word; it just goes from bad to worse.

Throwing water on the grease fire exacerbated it, causing the flames to spread.

excoriate to berate (eks-KOR-ee-āt)

If *excoriate* rubs you the wrong way, you've come

close to its original meaning, which was to remove the skin. It's not a word for the thin-skinned.

In the play Who's Afraid of Virginia Woolf? *the husband and wife constantly excoriate each other, denouncing one another for all manner of faults.*

exculpate to exonerate (EKS-kul-pāt)

Catholics of a certain age may remember saying "mea culpa" in the Latin Mass: "my fault." The *ex* takes the fault, or *culpa*, away. The word all but shouts NO GUILT.

The message on the bumper sticker was meant to exculpate. It read: "Don't blame me. I voted for my cockatoo."

exhort to urge strongly (egg-ZORT)

A polite way to say "badger"; it just won't let go.

Zealots of all stripes are good at exhorting their audiences, constantly admonishing them to act or think a certain way.

exsanguinate to drain of blood (eks-SAN-gwin-āt)

By itself, *sanguine*—indicating good color, thanks to blood flowing through the veins—means "optimistic." Which you wouldn't be if someone were about to exsanguinate you.

Always one to sink his teeth into his work, Dracula was a pro at exsanguinating when he latched on to a victim.

extirpate to destroy (EKS-tur-pāt)

Think *exterminate* and you'll know *extirpate*.

Hurricane Katrina extirpated New Orleans, wiping out much of the city.

finagle to achieve by trickery (fuh-NĀ-gull)

A word that goes well with "I managed to," because who doesn't want to succeed at least once by craft and cunning?

As the painted fence attests, Tom Sawyer had a sneaky way of getting friends to do his chores, always managing to finagle some work out of them.

foment to incite (fō-MENT)

This word is not so much a crowd-pleaser as a rabble-rouser—a real instigator. Where *foment* is found, trouble often follows.

The Boston Tea Party is a prime example of a rebellious bunch fomenting discord.

gambol to frolic or skip (GAM-bull)

Kick up those heels and those gams—meaning legs. *Gambol* is just a hop, a skip, and a romp away.

The young boys gamboled gleefully on the soft grass, without a care in the world.

garble to scramble (GAHR-bull)

This onomatopoeic word will add spice to your speech. It used to mean almost the opposite: to sort out and, in particular, to sift through different spices. But then the usage got garbled into its present meaning.

His mind was like a sieve, remembering little, and his testimony was so garbled that it was impossible to know what had actually happened.

immolate to kill in sacrifice (IM-uh-lāt)
> Where there's smoke, there's fire, and the same holds true of *immolate*. Steer clear of sacrificial pyres.

His barbecued chicken was so charred, his friends joked that he'd immolated the bird.

impugn to challenge (im-PYOON)
> If you sense a bit of pugnaciousness in *impugn*, you're right. *Impugn* is just waiting to catch someone in a lie.

Good investigative reporters are not afraid to impugn a subject's motives, hoping to uncover potential disparities or contradictions in a story.

impute to attribute to (im-PYOOT)
> *Imputing* may not make it so, but it sure makes it likely.

Because the hot dog was missing and the dachshund was smacking his lips, they imputed the disappearance of the one dog to the appearance of the other.

inculcate to indoctrinate (in-KUL-kāt)
> Repeat after us: *Inculcate* means "indoctrinate"; *inculcate* means "indoctrinate"; *inculcate* . . . Repetition is *inculcate*'s best friend. Once more now . . .

*Her parents inculcated her from an early age to say
please, thank you, and excuse me.*

mitigate to alleviate (MIT-uh-gāt)

Mitigate can't make it all better, but it won't be
quite as bad.

*Mitigate the problem and they won't want to litigate
the claim.*

mollify to pacify (MOLL-i-fī)

If you practice the politics of appeasement, you
know all about the calming, soothing quality of
mollify.

*Though the baby wanted the cookie, she was
mollified by a pacifier.*

obfuscate to confuse (OB-fus-kāt)

Betrayed, befuddled, and bewildered: that's what
obfuscating will render someone. It's a more
polite way of saying "baffle them with bull_____."

*If you can't convince 'em, confuse 'em. So much
obfuscation will have them ready to agree.*

parry to deflect (PAR-ee)

About the question you just asked—*Hey! Do you
see that star up there?* Back to your question—*Gee,
I wonder if it's been there all night.* Yes, we keep
evading the question, dodging it, parrying it. *But
back to that star . . .*

*Politicians become adept at parrying tough questions,
and by glossing over them, they minimize the risk of
alienating voters.*

pilfer to steal (PIL-fur)

> English pilfered this word from Old French, but like all pilfering, it's a slight of a swipe.

He pilfered a few pennies from the dish by the cash register.

prefigure to foreshadow (pree-FIG-yur)

> Doesn't it just figure? Yes, it often does, to the point of prefiguring, or suggesting, what will happen next.

In some respects the original Oxford English Dictionary *prefigured Wikipedia, with both reaching out to the larger community for information.*

prevaricate to equivocate (pri-VAR-i-kāt)

> *Truth* and *prevaricate* are not on friendly terms. *Prevaricate* spends its time evading the truth, misstating it, and straying from it. Let's just say it means "to lie," which it eventually comes around to meaning.

The defendant's answers were so vague that despite his oath to tell nothing but the truth, he was certainly prevaricating.

propitiate to appease (prō-PISH-ee-āt)

> When the goal is to propitiate, the outcome is often propitious, or favorable. The two words are etymological bedfellows.

An ambassador's role is often to propitiate, seeking conciliation in the name of goodwill.

purloin to steal (pur-LOYN)

It's okay to steal someone's heart, and even to steal the show, but the kind of thievery that *purloin* suggests holds no charm. It's just downright dishonest theft.

Someone must have purloined the confidential data, since it appeared on another report.

scuttle to abandon (SKUT-l)

If you've nixed it, scrapped it, or deep-sixed it, you've scuttled it.

When the boat started to take on water, we scuttled our plans for sailing to the island.

segue to transition smoothly (SEG-wā)

There's an old saying: "When one door closes, another one opens. But it sure is hell in the hallway." If only we could segue from one door to the next, we'd skip the hell in between. (Spell-check note: no, the correct spelling is *not* Segway—that's the scooter.)

The conversation segued from one topic to the next with no awkward pause.

surmise to guess (sur-MĪZ)

"To infer conjecturally" is to *surmise*, and we can surmise that this word has softened over the years from its etymological roots in the French *surmettre*, "to accuse."

From the feathers scattered across the cage, I surmised that the parrot had been preening while I was away.

vilify to defame (VIL-i-fī)

Trashing someone with malice in mind.

He was vile, full of bile, and took to vilifying the woman every chance he got, despite her fine reputation.

welter to wallow (WEL-tur)

It's never a good thing to be weltering. Often you're in need or turmoil, or on a (bad) roll, being tossed about in water or worse. Gimme shelter from welter.

The flash flood washed out the road at a ferocious rate, leaving the hikers weltering in mud.

whipsaw to trounce in two ways at once
(WIP-saw)

Whipsaw spells double trouble for the one being whipsawed, and quite possibly twice the satisfaction for the one doing the whipsawing. Literally, a whipsaw is a saw designed for two people to use, as when cutting a tree. Thus, to whipsaw is to cut someone down—not once but twice, and at the same time.

First he won my girlfriend's car in poker, then he won her heart. I was whipsawed.

winkle to pry open or out (WEENG-kul)

Ever try to coax a periwinkle out of its shell? No? Well, you've probably tried to pry a secret out of someone. Same thing: you're winkling.

Studs Terkel is an exceptional interviewer, a pro at winkling out the person behind the persona.

2

What's in a Name?

**Sum up friends (and foes)
in a snap**

Name-calling—when it's the right name you're calling someone—can be the ideal way to describe a person without ever needing an adjective.

arbiter judge (AHR-bi-tur)
> An arbiter is anything but arbitrary: arbiters wield significant power, much like their distant cousins, the umpires. Only it's not good form to shout "kill the arb."

Find the editor of a leading fashion magazine, and you've just met an arbiter of style.

blackguard a scoundrel (BLAG-urd)
> The word has a swagger to it, but its roots are in the humble kitchen servants who had to clean the pots and pans. They came to be called the black guard as a result of the dirty job.

Those dirty dogs—villains and blackguards, they are.

bounder an ill-mannered man (BOWN-dur)

A most British way of saying the guy's a jerk.
*A cad and a bounder would be many women's
estimation of Don Juan.*

cadre a closely knit group of qualified people
(KAH-drā)

A military word now wearing civvies, a cadre is
the group of people who form the framework of
a larger group because they have the experience,
passion, or both.

*The storm was severe enough that all the workers
stayed home except for a cadre of essential personnel.*

charlatan a fraud (SHAHR-luh-tun)

It's just a few etymological leaps from *charlatan*
to *chatter*, and most charlatans like to talk a good
line to cover up that quacking sound you hear.

*His improbable description of the bronze's history
pegged him as a charlatan: the statue was a fake.*

chattel a slave (CHAT-l)

It rhymes with *cattle* and was once interchange-
able with it. Livestock used to be considered a
most valuable portable property, just like a slave.

*They tried to cow her into submission, treating her
like chattel.*

contrarian one who thinks otherwise
(kun-TRAR-ee-un)

Contrarians have no use for conventional

wisdom. To the contrary, they take the opposing view.

Most everyone on Wall Street was predicting a bull market, but a few contrarians insisted it would be a bear.

cuckold a husband whose wife is unfaithful (KUK-uld)

Etymologically speaking, you have to be cuckoo to be a cuckold, but some of these birds honestly don't know their wives have flown the coop.

In the movie Unfaithful, *the husband flies into a rage when he learns he's a cuckold.*

denizen an inhabitant (DEN-i-zun)

Think of Norm and Cliff, habitués of the bar stools in the television series *Cheers*. The word means a regular, pumped up a few notches on the linguistic scale.

Denizens of the gym spend time there every day.

harpy a shrew (HAHR-pee)

You'd be ill-tempered and inclined to harp, too, if half of you were a woman and the other half a bird (even if you were just a myth).

In The Taming of the Shrew, *Katharina is a harpy, forever pitching fits and grumbling.*

harridan a nag (HA-ri-din)

Cross a nag with a hag and you get a harridan, but enough with these words that rag on women!

She was a scold and she was old, so they called Mrs.
Harrigan a harridan.

interlocutor one who participates in a dialogue
(in-tur-LAH-kyoo-tur)
>   As water is to rain, the interlocutor is to con-
>   versation. The word is a second cousin etymo-
>   logically to *loquacious*, which means "talkative."
The conference call had three interlocutors, so it was
a lively conversation.

interloper an intruder (IN-tur-lō-pur)
>   The party crasher is going to show up regard-
>   less, so you may as well make up a place card
>   labeled "interloper."
Seeing the "No Trespassing" sign, the interloper
thought, "That can't possibly mean me," as he opened
the gate.

mendicant a beggar (MEN-dik-unt)
>   If you have to beg, borrow, or steal, choose the
>   first option to be known as a mendicant.
Many friars of old were mendicants, owning no
property and depending on others.

minion a favorite (MIN-yun)
>   In school there's the brownnose. In business
>   there's the minion. Such a darling (and *darling*
>   is the French root) is low on the totem pole but
>   held in high esteem by the higher-ups. That's
>   because the little darling is such a brownnose.

Find a person with power and you'll find minions
ready to jump as high as they have to.

miscreant a villain (MISS-kree-unt)
    A case of a word morphing from bad to worse.
    A miscreant used to refer to an unbeliever. Now
    it's someone who is unbelievably bad.
There's nothing redeemable about him—he's a liar
and a miscreant.

mogul a powerful or wealthy person (MŌ-gull)
    A mogul is a magnate who's a magnet for those
    drawn to wealth and influence. Money not only
    talks, it rules.
The trend for many of today's moguls is to channel
their wealth and power into philanthropic causes.

mountebank an impostor (MOUN-tuh-bank)
    This notorious know-it-not pretends to be an
    expert. A mountebank used to mount a bench,
    the better to be heard by the crowd.
The doctor turned out to be a fake, a mountebank
who hawked a medicinal cure-all that was nothing
more than cough syrup.

mugwump one who remains neutral
(MUG-wump)
    Such a someone is usually in politics, where
    so-called neutrality isn't always the most politic.
    That may be why these neutral parties have
    been christened with such a clunker of a word.

Let's face it: *mugwump* (appropriated from the Algonquin) doesn't exactly trill off the tongue.
The mugwumps didn't vote on the casino issue, displeasing both sides.

nemesis an enemy or a source of trouble (NEM-uh-sis)

The polite way to say "pain in the ass."
The online world is the nemesis of those who hate technology.

philanderer a womanizer (fil-AN-dur-ur)

So many times *phil* signifies something positive—philanthropist, philosopher, Anglophile. But this Phil fools around with women and often cheats on his wife, so we've had our fill of this lover boy.
Women shouldn't pander to men who are philanderers.

poltroon a lazy coward (pul-TROON)

Poltroon packs a double insult, for a poltroon is not only gutless but a slug as well. No Purple Hearts here. The military reference is apt: poltroons were once draft dodgers who cut off their thumbs to avoid conscription. (Somewhere they found the courage to whack off their digits.)
Neither brave nor industrious, he was a poltroon.

polymath one schooled in many subjects (POL-ee-math)

The poster child of the liberal arts education

model, a polymath knows much about many
things.
He was a polymath, learned in many areas and
always learning about many more.

progenitor a founder (prō-JEN-i-tur)
Someone at the start of it all, especially an an-
cestral line.
Trace a family tree to its roots and you'll find the
progenitors.

provocateur a troublemaker (prō-vok-uh-TUR)
If you've ever been provoked into doing something dumb, blame it on the provocateur, or agi-
tator, who incited you.
He was a provocateur, always saying that the
woman didn't know how to use a gun, until finally
she turned her Smith & Wesson on him and fired.

rapscallion a rogue (rap-SKAL-yin)
A more emphatic way to say "rascal"; reserve it
for those who deserve it.
Robin Hood's merry men may have been
rapscallions, but their ne'er-do-well behavior
benefited the poor.

savant a sage (suh-VONT)
Save this word for describing the very, very
smart, and you'll never sound foolish.
Sir Thomas More was a savant, respected by both
theologians and academicians.

slattern a slovenly woman (SLAT-urn)
A slattern is a slut, with one more syllable for you to spit out contemptuously after muttering "sloppy" and "harlot" under your breath.
There's a difference between a flirt and a slattern, although the Puritans probably didn't think so.

stickler one who insists (STIK-lur)
Sticklers stickle. They're stubborn, and they have scruples. Their theme song is "You'll Do It My Way, Otherwise It's the Highway."
Henry Higgins of My Fair Lady *was a stickler for the correct pronunciation of words.*

sycophant a flatterer (SIK-uh-font)
A suck-up who doesn't know when to stop—although the derivation might give said suck-up pause: it's literally Greek for "fig shower." And as much as they may shower someone with praise, in reality sycophants don't give a fig.
The office sycophant is always first on the scene when the boss holds court.

thaumaturge a miracle worker (THAW-muh-turj)
Wonder Woman's real name was Thauma Woman, *thauma* being Greek for "wonder."
In the movie The Miracle Worker, *Helen Keller's remarkable teacher Annie Sullivan was portrayed as a true thaumaturge.*

wastrel a spendthrift (WĀS-trul)

Wasteful is the wastrel, especially when it comes to money.

He was such a wastrel he would never know wealth, as he spent even the money he didn't have.

3

In the Extreme

**As good as it gets, as bad
as it can be**

It seems to be human nature to describe situations, people, and things in the extreme—the best, the worst. English may be unparalleled when it comes to awarding superlatives.

anodyne soothing (AN-uh-dīn)
> The verbal equivalent of comfort food. No pain, just gain, with this stress-free word.

Her quiet, low, anodyne voice calmed his frayed nerves.

antipathy aversion (an-TIP-uhth-ee)
> *Antipathy* takes "dislike" to a whole new level, right up there with *repugnance*.

Some vegetarians are not just indifferent to meat; they have an antipathy toward it.

apotheosis deification, idealization
(uh-poth-ee-Ō-sis)
> Hero worship at its strongest: you're putting someone *waaaay* up there on the pedestal. It's

from the Greek for "to deify" (although, ironically, the Greeks sometimes let their gods topple off that pedestal).

This meringue is so divine, it's the apotheosis of a light dessert.

avaricious intensely desirous of wealth
(av-uh-RISH-us)

This is greed on the level of Gordon Gekko, the money-driven protagonist of the film *Wall Street* who famously pronounced that "greed is good." Bad, Gordon, bad.

Any guy that avaricious will never believe he has enough money; he'll always want more.

besmirch to tarnish or sully (bi-SMURCH)

Nowadays we're just as likely to say that so-and-so trashed someone, but *besmirch* says it with more indignation (and dignity).

By telling lies about me, you besmirch my reputation.

capstone acme (KAP-stōn)

A feather in the cap for *capstone*: it signifies a crowning achievement.

The highly successful iPod is a capstone in Apple's history.

chivalry gallantry (SHIV-ul-ree)

The French actor Maurice Chevalier, known for charming the ladies, had chivalry written all over him. His surname, Chevalier, is the root of *chivalry* and essentially means a knight on a horse. Just add shining armor.

Those to the manners born long for the days of chivalry.

copacetic highly satisfactory (kō-puh-SET-ik)
Old slang for the new slang of "it's all good." (But it sounds old-school.)

The sun is warm, the breeze is soft, and all is copacetic.

dereliction abandonment (dar-uh-LIK-shun)
If someone utters "willful and deliberate dereliction," they're in effect saying "dereliction, dereliction, dereliction." This is abandonment in the extreme.

Dereliction of duties is a serious offense in the military and elsewhere.

dissolute debauched (DISS-uh-loot)
Think of Oscar Wilde's *Picture of Dorian Gray* and you've nailed *dissolute*. Dorian's dissipated life eventually dissolves his face, and *dissolve* is at the root of *dissolute*.

His dissolute lifestyle showed in his face, his puffy eyes and broken capillaries signals of his debauchery.

egregious extraordinarily offensive (i-GREE-jus)
There's bad and there's beyond bad, so outstandingly so that you need a three-syllable word to say it.

His error in judgment was so egregious that it was impossible to fix the mistake.

epinician victorious (eh-pi-NISH-un)

> We won, and we're celebrating: that's what *epinician* is saying.

After winning the race, the track star ran an epinician lap around the field.

heinous abominable (HĀ-nis)

> Go right past "bad" and on to "horrific." That's how reprehensible *heinous* is.

Charles Manson's murders were some of the most heinous in modern history.

ignominy disgrace (IG-nuh-min-ee)

> The *nomin* part means "name," and when you shame your name, your reputation takes a serious hit.

The ignominy attached to being union busters proved too humiliating, so to avoid further disgrace, they joined the picket line.

internecine destructive on both sides (in-tur-NEE-seen)

> No good comes of *internecine*, as it's as damaging to one side as it is to the other.

Many divorces follow an internecine course, both parties saying or doing destructive things.

invidious offensive (in-VID-ee-us)

This word knows it's done its job if it's creating animosity, resentment, and ill will.

It was an invidious comment, intended to alienate, and all who heard it were offended.

laudatory praiseworthy (LAW-duh-tor-ee)

Laudatory is what graduates hope to see printed on their degrees, but in the original Latin of *cum laude.*

His leadership during the crisis was laudatory, and the people appreciated his wise decisions.

mendacity untruthfulness (men-DASS-i-tee)

After a certain age, shouting "Liar, liar, pants on fire" just doesn't work. Time to call it *mendacity.*

It was an outlandish tale of mendacity, with lie upon lie being told.

meretricious vulgar (mar-i-TRISH-us)

A meretricious person doesn't merit your attention—unless you like the flashy and gaudy.

Such meretricious behavior will not be tolerated here; we are a respectable establishment.

nefarious wicked (nuh-FAR-ee-us)

The *Nefarious* Witch of the West? Maybe not, but those wicked, wicked ways are what made her nefarious.

The actions of those involved in the pension scandal were nothing short of nefarious.

opprobrium disgrace or contempt
(uh-PRŌ-bree-um)

> This word is most definitely not above reproach. In fact, etymologically it's got *reproach* written all over it.

His conduct was so disgraceful that it brought opprobrium to his entire family.

paragon a model of perfection (PAR-uh-gon)

> When they're people, paragons are usually persons a lot of us love to hate (what makes *them* so perfect?). When they're objects, like the 100-carat flawless diamond that goes by this description— well, then they're positively peerless.

She was a paragon of dietary virtue, never succumbing to dessert, and we found such perfect control perfectly maddening. Another scoop of double-fudge butter crunch, please.

parlous dangerous (PAHR-lus)

> Where there's *parlous*, there's "perilous." Danger awaits.

The journey was parlous, the travelers constantly on their guard.

perfidy treachery (PUR-fi-dee)

> Utterly untrustworthy is *perfidy*, a calculated breach of faith (the *fide* embedded in the word is Latin for "faith").

The perfidy of the traitors knew no bounds; they would never be forgiven.

salacious lustful (suh-LĀ-shus)

Think "jump your bones" to remember this word—its origin is in *leaping*.

The man had a salacious look on his face as he eyed the sexy woman.

sanguine cheery (SANG-win)

To those lucky sanguine souls, life is rosy, down to the rosy red in their cheeks. That rosy color means good circulation or flow of blood. In medieval physiology, blood, or *sanguine*, was one of the body's four humors that determined temperament. Today a sanguine person is considered to be in good humor.

She was such a sanguine sort, always saying that life was just a bowl of cherries.

scabrous scandalous (SKAB-rus)

Rough stuff is *scabrous*, a word that originally meant just that—"rough"—and has come to mean "squalid and nasty." Think of *scab*, and that's roughly along the lines of *scabrous*.

It was scabrous material, with excessive violence, and the parents would not let their children read it.

scurrilous vulgar and abusive (SKUR-uh-lus)

A high-handed word for describing a lowlife. You can practically hear the indignation as you say it.

The comedian was coarse and foul-mouthed, and such a scurrilous act did not play well with the audience.

succor assistance (SUK-ur)

Once a form of *sugar*, it's now a soothing-sounding way of saying help or aid. Sweet.

Her wise counsel gave him succor when he most needed it, and he was grateful for her help.

symbiosis a mutually beneficial relationship (sim-bee-Ō-sis)

Something of a you-scratch-my-back, I'll-scratch-yours arrangement, whereby two organisms help each other live. It's common in the plant and animal worlds but works for humans, too.

Networking is a form of symbiosis, with people sharing contacts and information to help one another get ahead.

turpitude depravity (TUR-pi-tood)

Best used when you can adopt a holier-than-thou tone, indicating that you could never be so base.

The lies those con artists told were a shameful example of moral turpitude.

4

One-Syllable Wonders

Keep it short and snappy

Who says a word must be long in order for its user to sound sophisticated? When it comes to syllables, the true sophisticate knows the power of one.

blurb a testimonial (BLURB)

"Will you blurb my book?" is a common plea among writers when they're looking for endorsements for their book. *Blurb* works as both a noun and a verb. Gelett Burgess (1866–1951)—the writer who penned the famous "Purple Cow" poem—coined this word. Here is Burgess's blurb for his own book:

Don't let my adjectives astute
Your peace of mind disturb;
It's "bold," it's "clever" and it's "cute,"
And so is this my blurb!

brusque blunt (BRUSK)

Hear how abruptly this single clipped syllable ends? It is what it sounds like: *blunt.*

His manner was brusque, given to cutting people off
before they finished their—

carp to criticize (KAHRP)

Pick, pick, pick: that's all this word knows how
to do. What a nag!

The customer carped so much about how poorly the
product worked that the salesperson offered a free
upgrade.

corps a close-knit group (KOR)

This military term is at home in the civilian world
as well, and suggests a body of people who func-
tion as one.

The volunteers were a special corps of people,
always able to work together and ready to support
one another.

daft silly (DAFT)

The British are fond of this word, possibly because they've had their share of the crazy and
foolish (spaghetti on toast, for starters). Say "a
bit daft" and you'll add that nice British crust
to it.

Many thought the high-flying Richard Branson a bit
daft when he named his airline Virgin.

dearth a scarcity (DURTH)

Something the English language will never be
accused of when it comes to words or interesting stories behind them. *Dearth* got its start with

dear, in the sense of "costly" and hence sometimes "scarce."

There is a surplus of gossip and a dearth of real news.

droll amusing (DRŌLL)

Droll is fun to have around. It keeps good company with *witty*, *wry*, and *whimsical*.

His droll humor often caught her off guard, making her laugh in unexpected places.

eke to acquire with difficulty (EEK)

So tough is it to eke out the meaning of *eke* in one word that it takes several words to get the point across. Suffice it to say that *eke* is hard work.

For the most part, the people of Appalachia manage to eke out a simple living, but no more.

fey slightly unreal (FĀ)

Hey, *fey*, what do you say? Namely, that this wisp of a word can go either way: toward the eccentric or strange, or toward the magical and fairylike.

Fairy tales are filled with the fey—characters sometimes forbidding and other times magical.

flout to scorn (FLOWT)

When it comes to contempt and disdain, *flout* knows how to dish it out.

Bostonians are famous for flouting their traffic laws. (What laws? ask the Bostonians.)

fug stale air (FUG)

Ugh, it's a fug. Somebody open a window and freshen up this stale air.

He was in a funk, and the fact that his room was a fug that hadn't seen fresh air in days made it worse.

guile cunning (GĪL)

Rhymes with *wile*, which is what guile is full of.

In John Steinbeck's East of Eden, *Cathy appears to be without guile, but beneath her sweet face lurk deceit and treachery.*

hew to adhere to (HYOO)

Pronounced similarly to *achoo*, and the level of conformity that *hew* suggests is nothing to sneeze at.

Nonconformists hew to no party line, forever seeking their own paths.

hone to sharpen (HŌN)

If you want to sharpen your linguistic skills, know when to use *hone* ("to sharpen") and when to use *home in on* ("to zero in on").

After honing her presentation skills, she homed in on the topics that her speech would cover.

jibe to be in sync with (JĪB)

Let's all agree that *jibe* is the word that describes "accord" . . . and that's no jive.

The accounts of the two key witnesses didn't jibe, and because they differed so markedly, the prosecution won its case.

kine cows (KĪN)

> We have our friends at NPR to thank for using this word on one of their shows. Who knew that cows were kine? Although "till the kine come home" takes some getting used to.

The Ben & Jerry's ice cream brand has long been keen on kine, even showing graphics of cows on some of its labels.

limn to describe (LIM)

> A slender slip of a word that's at home in the most elegant writing, it means to draw or portray. It's a not-so-distant cousin of *illuminate*.

Poets can limn a vivid picture of a place in just a few words.

loath unwilling (LŌTH)

> If you say "I don't want to," you'll sound like a whiner. If you say "I'm loath to do it," you'll sound more mature, self-possessed, and in control—a literary whiner.

She was loath to loaf around the lodge all day, preferring to be out on the slopes.

mien appearance (MEEN)

> The text-message spelling of *demeanor*.

The queen has a regal mien.

mine to extract (MĪN)

> We tend to think that *mine* is only for miners, but what's theirs is ours: next time you find yourself digging or delving for information, you're mining.

She mined every book on rubies she could find,
looking for a few good gems of information.

moot irrelevant (MOOT)

Whenever you find yourself thinking you're
over it, or longing to tell a particular person
to *get* over it, that's when to say, "It's a moot
point." Just don't confuse *moot* with *mute*—
that's dumb.

Since he no longer had a car, the question of
renewing his driver's license was moot.

parse to deconstruct (PAHRSS)

It's often sentences that have the honor of being
parsed, with each word broken down according
to its part of speech, its use in the sentence, and
so on. If you're really, really desperate on a Sat-
urday night, give it a try.

One way to appreciate certain poetry is to parse it,
analyzing how each word relates to the others.

pelf wealth of questionable origin (PELF)

Ill-gotten gains is more like it. Think *pilfered* and
you'll be close. Or pirates with their booty.

Some might say that the staggering profits of the oil
companies are like pelf, wealth not so much earned
as squeezed out of consumers.

plumb to fathom (PLUM)

Plumbing is not just for plumbers. It's also for
digging deep into thoughts and emotions.

The psychiatrist plumbed the depths of the patient's emotions, trying to fathom such destructive behavior.

queue a line (KYOO)

The Brits, that orderly bunch, are fond of this word, and heaven help you if you jump one of their queues. For Americans, *queue* saves us the problem of whether we should say we're standing *on* line (as New Yorkers do) or *in* line (like the rest of us).

There was such a long queue to get into the exhibit that we worried about getting in before the museum closed.

rogue a scoundrel, a scamp, a deviant—and sometimes an elephant (RŌG)

Rogue can mean a real scoundrel, a playful one, a vagrant, something that deviates from the norm . . . or a bad-tempered elephant that's broken with the herd.

Among all the shiny pennies that tumbled out was one rogue coin, not coppery like all the rest.

roil to anger (ROYL)

You know that person who's such a royal pain? That person roils you.

She was always stirring up trouble and then running off, roiling the rest of the group.

rube an unsophisticated person (ROOB)

A word of advice: don't name your son Reuben lest he turn into a rube.

He was a rube from Hicksville who'd never heard of a Reuben sandwich.

rue to regret (ROO)

This is not the "I regret to inform you" regret. This one goes deeper and is more genuine.

He rued the day he sold his boat, as he longed to be on the water again.

scree loose rock (SKREE)

Next time you find yourself on the slope of a mountain, tripping over the loose stones underfoot, what you want to be cursing out is called scree. The word derives from *landslide*. You just may want to come down off that mountain now . . .

The hikers found it hard going across the scree, as the loose rock covered most of the mountainside.

screed a long harangue (SKREED)

If diatribes aren't your vibe, steer clear of this long, monotonous, monotonously long—and did we mention monotonous?—discussion.

It wasn't so much an essay as a screed, a long and windy complaint about the damage the windmills would do.

scrim a transparent curtain (SKRIM)

Think of a veil, both revealing and concealing. That's a scrim, but on a larger scale. It works metaphorically as well.

It was as if a scrim of sadness had covered her face.

skunk to defeat resoundingly (SKUNK)

We all know the word for the stinky little creature, but there's a reason—linguistically, anyway—to love it. *Skunk* is one of the few words that Noah Webster could crow about being specific to American English (because, of course, nobody else had the stinky little creature). Be a good American and try using the word as a verb.

The other team skunked us in the game; we couldn't score a point.

slew a large number (SLOO)

There's a ton of, a bunch of, a whole lot of—but *a slew of* makes the ear sit up and take notice. Plus, it saves your having to figure out exactly how many are in that big bunch.

I found a slew of bills waiting for me after my vacation.

squib a short piece in a newspaper or magazine (SKWIB)

Another word would be *filler*. Newspapers and magazines are filled with these short, punchy pieces. Think of them as sight bites.

The New Yorker *is famous for its cartoons but also known for its squibs, which are usually humorous or thought provoking.*

suss to figure out (SUSS)

Thank the Brits for figuring out how to use *suspect* in such a sibilant-sounding fashion.

Having sussed out the source of the blaze, the fire chief suspected arson.

tome a scholarly book (TŌM)

A short word for what is invariably a *lonnnng* work, often just one of several volumes.

Encyclopedias are tomes that only an intrepid few have ever read through.

wan weak or melancholy (WAHN)

If one is the loneliest number, *wan* is the saddest single syllable.

Her wan smile betrayed how sad she was about leaving.

weal the general well-being (WEEL)

A word not oft heard (archaic, sniff some dictionaries), and yet it carries none of the baggage that *welfare* does. A commonweal once referred to a commonwealth, which is what states such as Massachusetts and Pennsylvania officially are.

The U.S. Constitution is a document that addresses the common weal.

wile trickery (WĪL)

> *Wile* can beguile. This trickery is more of the disarming than the dangerous kind, closer to magic than to malevolence. P.S. Did you know the correct expression is *wile away* [the afternoon], not *while away*? (Neither did we.)

She used every wile she possessed to try to win his heart.

wont habit (WAHNT, WUNT, or WŌNT)

> Just about any way you want to pronounce *wont* will work. Since you can't go wrong saying it, may as well get in the habit of using it.

It was his wont to start his day at sunrise, and he was so accustomed to doing this that he didn't want or need an alarm clock.

wrest to extract forcefully (REST)

> There's no rest for those who wrest—it takes a lot of elbow grease to take something with the force that *wrest* implies.

After an intense scuffle, he was able to wrest the incriminating document from his would-be blackmailer.

5

The Classics

**Get to the Latin and Greek
root of the matter**

If language had DNA, Latin and Greek would be critical components of the English genetic code. Use a few of these words from antiquity in everyday conversation to elevate your discussions.

augur to predict (AW-gur)

A direct swipe from the Roman word for the officials, or augurs, who did the foretelling. Who knew the word would last so long?

A red sky in the morning augurs the chance of rain.

catharsis a purge or release (ku-THAHR-sis)

The Greeks, who coined the word, knew a thing or two about letting go. Okay, everyone, on cue: exhale.

Being able to unload her worries onto her friend was a welcome catharsis.

caveat a warning (KAV-ee-ot)

The Romans, who were often on their guard, gave us this cautionary word.

Caveat emptor *is a famous Latin saying, meaning "Let the buyer beware."*

chimerical wildly fanciful (kuh-ME-ri-kull)

Imagine a fire-breathing creature that's part goat, part lion, and part dragon. That's not only chimerical—it's Chimera, the Greek mythological creature that spawned this word for imagination gone amok.

A scientist's experiments are sometimes considered chimerical by laypeople, but there's nothing fanciful about them: every step is deliberate.

encomium praise (en-KŌ-mee-um)

Let us now praise a word that gives us another way to say *praise*, and knows how to party as well. The root is in the Greek word for "revelry."

Praise be, the teachers lavished my son with encomiums for being a model student.

ephemera something short-lived (i-FEM-ur-uh)

"Here today, gone tomorrow" is the stuff of ephemera, as *hemera* is Greek for "day." (Although try telling this to collectors of antique ephemera, who usually keep the stuff for years.)

At the end of each day he would empty his pockets, removing gum wrappers, scribbled notes, and other ephemera.

ex nihilo out of nothing (eks NEE-uh-lō)

An old Roman would probably say *ex nihilo nihil*

fit: out of nothing, nothing comes. It was the ancient precursor, perhaps, to *garbage in, garbage out.*

The bursting of the dot-com bubble was a lesson in ex nihilo: that out of nothing, you eventually get nothing.

factotum a worker with many duties
(fak-TŌ-tum)

Here is the multitasker extraordinaire, the jack-of-all-trades and master of many.

Those who call themselves chief cook and bottle washer are factotums by another name.

gravitas seriousness (GRAHV-i-tahss)

Become bilingual in an instant with *gravitas*. It's Latin straight up for "solemnity."

His subdued manner and solemn tone conveyed a certain gravitas.

hegemony dominance (hi-JEM-uh-nee)

In global politics, the leader of the pack among countries or states gets to claim hegemony.

Some say the American hegemony of the twentieth century is now being challenged, as other countries begin to take the lead in the global arena.

hoi polloi the masses (HOY puh-LOY)

High on the snob meter, *hoi polloi* allows you to show just how high above all that riffraff and those commoners you are. The trick is to always say *hoi polloi*, never *the hoi polloi*, as *hoi* is Greek for "the."

The Gilded Age mansions of Newport were far removed from the city's wharves, ensuring that the Astors and the Vanderbilts did not have to mix with hoi polloi.

hubris excessive pride (HYOO-briss)

Today we might say *cocky, arrogant,* and *know-it-all*. The Greeks combined those with the consequences that would befall such excessive pride: the gods would get you. Just ask Oedipus.

His hubris was so great that even though he had perfected the new parachute design, it hadn't occurred to him that he would need one when he jumped from the plane.

impediment a hindrance (im-PED-uh-munt)

The moral of *impediment* is to travel light. *Impedimenta*, its Latin grandparent, means "luggage." How did those old Romans know what a pain a carry-on can be?

Peter Greenberg, the well-known Travel Detective, doesn't let his baggage be an impediment to his travels. To keep it from getting in the way, he sends it on ahead.

imprimatur approval (im-pri-MAH-tur)

Used to be only the pope or his representatives could give this kind of written blessing, signaling that something could be printed. But when blessed with such a useful word, why not let it work for the laity, too? We just usually call such approvals *blurbs* or *reviews*.

Our favorite film critic has given the movie a thumbs-up, so now that it has that imprimatur, we'll see it.

incunabula the first printed books
(in-kyoo-NAH-byoo-luh)

The word is almost as rare as the books it describes: these were books printed before 1500. If you have any incunabula lying around, get thee to an appraiser.

Gutenberg Bibles are considered incunabula, since they were printed in the mid-1400s.

inter alia among other things (IN-tur AHL-ee-uh)

It's Latin, so inter alia, you'll sound smart if you use this expression—and even smarter if you abbreviate it in your writing: int. al.

The grocery list was long and included, inter alia, grapes, apples, and pears.

interregnum a period when activity is suspended
(in-tur-REG-num)

In its most literal use, *interregnum* refers to the time between sovereigns' reigns—hence the regal *regnum*. But its majestic tone works outside palace walls, too.

Finding himself with two months between plays, the actor used the interregnum to read up on the character he would next be portraying.

magister dixit thus spoke the master
(mih-GIS-ter DEEK-sit)

Or in more modern parlance, "Yes, boss."
After the earl of the manor gave the day's orders to his butler, the butler turned to the rest of the staff and said, "Magister dixit, and we must see to all his wishes."

mea culpa acknowledgment of fault
(MĀ-uh KUL-puh)

If it's hard for you to fess up in English, announce it in Latin instead.
After forgetting to bring the salad, the server returned to the table with his mea culpa.

miasma poison air (mī-AZ-muh)

Pollution in the extreme, and a word you can use metaphorically as well as literally.
The two sides hated each other and created a miasma of distrust and accusation when they came together.

minuscule tiny (MIN-uh-skyool)

The word derives from *minus* rather than *mini.* That's how you'll remember to spell it correctly.
The opals were minuscule—you could barely see the stones in the setting.

noli me tangere do not touch
(NŌ-lee mā TAN-guh-ree)

The Latin equivalent of "Back off, buster," although the Romans would have said, "Touch me not." And not just literally: it also means "no meddling."

He's aloof and standoffish, with an air of noli me tangere that keeps others at arm's length.

pandemic a disease affecting a large portion of the world (pan-DEM-ik)

A gloom-and-doom term of epic proportion. An epidemic affects many and is bad. A pandemic affects many more and is much worse.

The Black Death of the fourteenth century was a pandemic, sweeping through much of Europe and killing more than 20 million people.

paterfamilias the head of the household (PĀ-ter-fuh-MIL-ee-us)

Join *pater* (father) with *familias* (family), and you have an entry for a linguistic artifact—not because it's Latin but because the idea that only a father can be the head honcho at home is so last century.

Robert Young played the paterfamilias on the old television show Father Knows Best.

plebeian common, lowly (pluh-BEE-un)

Put on your best toga when you say this, as *plebeian* was what the highfalutin Romans called the unpretentious common folks. It's still a handy way of sounding high-handed when calling someone coarse and unrefined.

He had a way of looking down his patrician nose at the rest of us, who were clearly plebeian in his eyes and too common to bother with.

quondam former (KWON-dum)
  The Latin word for this is . . . *quondam*! See how easy it is to talk like Cicero and the boys?
My quondam confidante spilled my secret, so we no longer speak.

quotidian daily; everyday (kwō-TID-ee-un)
  Combine *quotus* (how many) and *dies* (day), and you have an out-of-the-ordinary word that takes the monotony out of the day-in, day-out.
The quotidian nature of a nine-to-five workweek makes us long for the unexpected.

sub rosa private or confidential (sub RŌ-zuh)
  Keep this under your hat: a rose in ancient times was a symbol of secrecy; hence, *sub rosa*, or "under the rose," means "in secret."
The two met sub rosa, so that no one would know what they were discussing.

tabula rasa a clean slate (TAB-yoo-luh RAHZ-uh)
  Literally, Latin for "scraped tablet," but used figuratively to mean "blank slate," as with a young mind or a new beginning.
Young children are impressionable, their minds a tabula rasa for what they hear (and overhear) adults say.

xeric adapted to a dry environment (ZEER-ik)
Think zero water and that's *xeric*. Environmentalists see green when they see this word because it suggests water conservation.

A xeric garden makes sense in the desert Southwest, since this vegetation doesn't need much water.

6

Imports

Souvenirs from abroad

English—the consummate sponge of a language—has absorbed words from many other languages. Try these when you're casting about for *le mot juste*—just the right word.

aficionado a fervent enthusiast
(uh-fish-yuh-NAHD-ō)
 If you like it, you're a fan. If you love it, you're an aficionado. It's a fancy way of saying how passionately you care about something from a language that's full of passion: Spanish.
He is such a fishing aficionado that he makes his own lures.

agitprop propaganda (AJ-it-prop)
 Agitprop is derived from a string of Russian syllables as long as the Russian winters. Just think *agitate* and *propaganda*, both of which Russia was well versed in during the Communist era, when the word came into fashion.

Some would say that certain activist groups dispense nothing but agitprop.

anomie instability (AN-uh-mee)

Sociologists often use this French word to describe societies whose values are suffering a nervous breakdown. It seems to have happened a lot since 1596, when the word first appeared.

There comes a point when most generations look upon the next as wallowing in a state of anomie.

avatar an embodiment (AV-uh-tahr)

This word had a life long before the website "Second Life" made it popular, and its ancient Hindu meaning lives on: "an incarnation."

The unbeatable racehorse was the avatar of a Triple Crown winner.

brio gusto (BREE-ō)

Lively, spirited, and vivacious: that's Italian, and that's *brio*. Use it in a like manner.

Every year, the Rockettes perform at the Macy's Thanksgiving Day Parade with their customary high-kicking brio.

canard a hoax or rumor (kuh-NAHRD)

Only a silly goose gets caught in a canard. The word is French for "duck," and this use goes back to the French expression *vendre un canard à moitié*, or "to half-sell a duck"—which is, of course, impossible.

For a while a canard was flying around that the

singer had canceled the performance, but it wasn't true. He'd merely ducked out of rehearsal early.

contretemps an embarrassing event
(KON-truh-tahn)

> If Lemony Snicket were French, his *Series of Unfortunate Events* might be known as a string of contretemps.

After the contretemps in the cloakroom left her holding the wrong jacket, she was so humiliated that she never checked her coat again.

coup de foudre something extraordinary
(KOO duh FOOD)

> For the French, whose expression this is, that something extraordinary is often love at first sight, which is how you might see the term used. That's why they'll always have Paris.

When the American chef Julia Child discovered French cooking, the result was a coup de foudre.

debacle a resounding defeat (di-BAHK-ull)

> Let this French word ricochet off your palate, as if it's automatically revealing just how crushing, ruinous, and disastrous a downfall it is.

The game was a debacle. The (Dodgers/Yankees/ Red Sox/pick your team) lost 21–zip.

demimonde women of questionable reputation
(DEM-ee-mond)

> What Carrie Bradshaw and her *Sex and the City* cohorts would have been labeled back in the

day when promiscuity was apt to put a big red
A on your chest. *Oui*, it is French.
Sexual indiscretions in the Victorian era could result
in well-born women becoming part of the
demimonde.

denouement outcome, resolution (dā-noo-MON)
A complicated word for how the story ends,
best used when it's been a complicated story.
Think of it as an untying of a knotty situation,
which takes you close to the word's French and
Latin roots.
Given the complexity of the story, the denouement
came as little surprise.

dernier cri the latest (dar-nee-ar KREE)
In English we have the *last word*. In French they
have the *last cry*. Who better than the French to
use a phrase that means "the latest" to describe
the newest in fashion?
Fashion magazines are filled with the dernier cri
in design, but many of these last words won't last
long.

dishabille partially undressed (diss-uh-BEEL)
A buttoned-up word that means "half-dressed."
If it weren't so polite (and so French), it might
even indicate disheveled.
The milkman caught me dishabille, so I dressed him
down for not having any cream.

echt authentic (EKT)

Americans might say "the real McCoy," but the Germans have a more cryptic way of saying "genuine."

This handbag is echt Chanel, not an imitation.

eminence grise the power behind the power
(EM-uh-nunss GREEZ)

In the politics of power, there are the people in charge, and then there are the people in charge of those in charge. These last are often the more powerful. Cardinal Richelieu's secretary was one such behind-the-scenes power broker. His dull-colored robes (*grise* means "gray") gave us this colorful French expression, which is often cloaked in intrigue.

Behind many a powerful person is an eminence grise, pulling the strings and calling the shots.

ennui boredom (on-WEE)

That's boredom with a capital *B*. Even (*yawn*) thinking about this French word makes us (*zzzz*) listless.

In college it was the fashion to be in a constant state of ennui, allowing nothing to excite us.

en plein air outdoors (on plen AR)

Americans go outside, Italians go *al fresco*, the French go *en plein air*. A particularly useful term if you're trying to impress an Old World wine snob.

Come, mon ami, let us savor a glass of this 1996
Pavillon Rouge du Château Margaux en plein air, so
that we can enjoy the night sky.

ersatz artificial (UR-zats)

Why is the *s* pronounced like a *z*, and the *z* like
an *s*, in *ersatz*? Zat's because it's a German word.
"Send in the reinforcements" is pretty much
how this Teutonic term got its anglicized start.
But reinforcements aren't quite the real thing,
are they? Hence, they're artificial.

There are lots of ersatz sweeteners available, but
nothing is quite as sweet as sugar.

folie à deux a shared delusion (foll-ee ah DE)

It takes two to tango, and also to become entan-
gled in a *folie à deux*. It's French for a double
dose of folly.

Bonne and Clyde had a folie à deux that their
spectacular bank heists would forever elude the law.

force majeure a catastrophic occurrence beyond
human control (forss muh-ZHUR)

"The vacuum cleaner ate my report" is not a
force majeure. "The earthquake swallowed our
building and my report with it" is. The French
term is often used in legally binding contracts as
an out clause in the event of a natural disaster.

The contract included a clause that removed any
penalty for late delivery in the event of a force
majeure, as that would be out of everyone's control.

imbroglio a complicated state of affairs
(im-BRŌL-yō)
> When you're embroiled in an imbroglio, you're
> in a tangle, as any Italian knows, so don't be sur-
> prised if you get caught up in a bitter disagree-
> ment.

The imbroglio surrounding the Watergate break-in
prompted two young reporters of the time, Bob
Woodward and Carl Bernstein, to try to untangle the
situation and get to the truth.

impresario a director or producer
(im-pruh-SAHR-ee-ō)
> A producer produces; an impresario does it with
> flair, style, passion, and drive. Not for nothing is
> this word's root Italian.

Federico Fellini was an impresario of film, creating
such classics as La Dolce Vita.

insouciant carefree (in-SOO-shunt)
> Not a worry, nary a care—who lives like this?
> Settle for a few insouciant moments when you
> can get them. Oh, and if you care, the word is
> French.

Children at play are insouciant bundles of energy,
with worries the furthest things from their minds.

joie de vivre exuberance (zhwah duh VEEV-ruh)
> "The joy of living" is the literal translation of this
> French saying, and if you had the good meals that
> the French enjoy every day, you'd be happy, too.

Her smile and the sparkle in her eye conveyed a joie de vivre that made you happy to be around her.

jolie laide unconventionally attractive
(zho-lee LĀD)

> *Merci* to the French for finding a pretty way to describe a not-so-pretty woman as being appealing nevertheless. Equal-opportunity note: if it's a guy, he's *joli laid*.

Diana Vreeland, the legendary editor of Vogue *magazine, was not beautiful but rather jolie laide, her distinctive looks appealing in their own right.*

juggernaut an overpowering force (JUG-ur-nawt)

> English lifted this word from Sanskrit, and it's a fitting theft, as the English-speaking world has often been perceived by developing nations as being a juggernaut of power.

The Arctic air was a juggernaut of cold, blasting its way across the Great Plains.

koan a verbal puzzle that's used as a mental stimulus (KŌ-un)

> This Zen Buddhist technique is used in meditation. A koan is a puzzle that's paradoxical: it's a stimulus that's calming. By pondering the koan, you take your mind away from other thoughts. It's a Japanese word that means, in part, "matter for thought."

Puzzles that provide a mental stimulus for adults include the well-known crosswords and the lesser-known koans.

macabre ghastly (muh-KAHB)

Death and decay dance around this French word, which is usually defined in terms of *danse macabre*, the "dance of death." Don't try to learn the steps.

The macabre scene on the field of Gettysburg after the Civil War battle was one of death and despair.

majordomo the head of staff (MĀ-jur-DŌ-mō)

Major bossy is more like it. Thank the Spanish for the majordomo: the one in charge, who sees that things get done.

Recently there's been a resurgence in butlering as a profession, and the head butler is considered the majordomo of the household.

mandarin a high government official (MAN-duh-rin)

Forget those canned orange slices. Use this Sanskrit term to describe top officials who sometimes appear smarter than they are.

With its abundance of government officials, Washington, D.C., may well have more mandarins per square mile than any other American city.

manqué failed or unfulfilled (mon-KĀ)

Not so much a wannabe as a coulda-been, often if only the person woulda tried harder. Somehow in French it doesn't sound so bad.

Everyone told her what a beautiful voice she had, but the singer manqué was never brave enough to audition.

mise en place to put in place (meez on PLAHSS)

Kitchen Confidential chef Anthony Bourdain introduced us to this French expression, which he shorthands to *meez*. It's the way a good cook gets set up to cook, all ingredients and utensils organized and ready, mind focused. This is not the time to worry about the mess you're about to make.

If you have your meez right, it means you have your head together, you are "set up," stocked, organized, ready with everything you need and are likely to need for the tasks at hand.

—Anthony Bourdain, *Les Halles Cookbook*

poseur a pretender (pō-ZUR)

The fancy French way of describing someone who puts on airs, all the better to be filled with hot air.

He was a chronic poseur, always assuming a posh British accent and wearing tweeds.

précis a summary (PRĀ-see)

Although the word is French, it's been popular with British university students for years. It sounds more impressive than *short report*.

Her concise précis of the book was much more readable than the book itself.

raconteur a storyteller (rah-kon-TUR)

Every party, talk show, and family should have at least one member who can turn a mere anecdote into a marvelous story. Even if that person isn't French, he or she will be a raconteur.

In his role as raconteur, Mark Twain would tell his daughters stories using objects on the mantel.

sangfroid composure (song-FWAH)

Hemingway called it grace under pressure; the French call it sangfroid (literally, "cold blood"). It's that cool-as-a-cucumber calmness that makes some people appear imperturbable when they should feel stressed.

Good quarterbacks have sangfroid, keeping a cool head even when the heat is on.

Schadenfreude delight over another's misfortune (SHAH-dun-froy-duh)

Like the person you must invite to the party, this is the German word that word-book writers must include in theirs. The hope is that if we all see it enough, we'll eventually figure out how to spell it. Think sweet and sour: someone else is having a tough go of it and you're reveling in it. Oh come on, we've all done it.

His Schadenfreude in seeing that the player who replaced him was having a rough time was vindication for being benched.

Schilderwald too many signs (SHIL-dur-wald)

This German term is a bit like saying you can't see the trees for the forest, for it means "sign forest." If you've ever driven on Route 192 around

Orlando, Florida, and been bombarded by bill-
boards at every blink, you know such a forest.
*The road was a veritable Schilderwald, the signs
blocking much of the scenery.*

shivaree a mock serenade (SHIV-uh-ree)
Those spoons clanking on goblets at wedding
receptions are a toned-down version of a shivaree. The custom originated in France as a bawdy
way to harass newlyweds by serenading them
with noisemakers. The original French word may
have come from the Latin for "headache," which
is often the by-product of a shivaree.
*The gala began as a tribute to the honoree and ended
as a good-natured roast, the hosts delivering a
hilarious shivaree.*

soupçon a small amount (soop-SON)
Next time you're tempted to say *smidgen*, say
soupçon instead, and you'll sound just the tiniest
bit French.
*The recipe called for a soupçon of salt, so we put in
just a pinch.*

succès d'estime a critical but not popular
success (suk-SĀ des-TEEM)
To bean counters, ain't no such thing as *succès* if
it's only *d'estime*. But this French phrase can be
a tactful way to say that the movie bombed at
the box office even though the critics loved it.
For a number of artists, their work is a succès

*d'estime during their lifetime, drawing praise only
from the few. Only later, when the artists are long
gone, does their work gain popular favor.*

tour de force an amazing feat (toor duh FORSS)
Good happens often, great happens occasion-
ally, but a tour de force happens rarely. Save this
French find for those rare instances and you'll
get the maximum impact from this force.
*Her performance was a tour de force, leaving the
audience first gasping and then wildly applauding.*

über extreme or ultimate (OO-bur)
You could say you were way busy or you could
say you were über busy. Try saying *über*, and
you'll sound so busy that people might leave
you alone—especially if they know the meaning of this German word.
The über athlete relishes extreme sports.

umami an exceptional, delicious taste (oo-MOM-ee)
Just as the Japanese have done cars one better,
so have they done taste one better. *Umami* means
it doesn't just taste good—it's the essence of
delicious.
*Edamame might be said to possess umami, as its
texture gives it an uncommonly good taste.*

Zeitgeist the character of an era (ZĪT-gīst)
It takes several words in English to describe this
phenomenon that German manages to say in

just one. *Zeit* is "time" and *geist* is "spirit": the spirit of the time.

The Zeitgeist of the 1960s was one of youthful rebellion against just about anything and almost everyone over thirty.

7
Literary Flair

Worthy of the finest salons

No doubt about it: these are those highbrow words you're apt to encounter in literature and wonder what they mean. Now you'll know.

addlepated muddled (AD-l-pā-ted)
> A more literary way of saying "lamebrained" or "emptyheaded." *Pate* is an old word for "top of the head."

What kind of addlepated thinking equates war with peace?

albeit although (all-BEE-it)
> *Although* is a perfectly good word for "even though," albeit sometimes you want another word to keep things interesting. Chaucer would choose *albeit*, but he would write it as three words: *al + be + it.*

It's a rainy, albeit warm, day.

archetype prototype (AHR-kuh-tīp)

The archetype is the quintessential ideal, often a difficult type to live up to.

The doting grandma knitting sweaters is the archetype of the grandparent.

assignation a lovers' meeting (ass-ig-NĀ-shun)

Now, here's a word that understands romance. It all but whispers "tryst." This meeting will be an affair to remember.

When the heroes of the film Sleepless in Seattle *rendezvous in New York, they're mirroring Cary Grant's assignation with his lover in another film.*

assize verdict, decree (uh-SĪZ)

The word conjures up images of British courts and powdered wigs, so hear ye this: as long as there are edicts, there will be assizes.

James Kilpatrick has been known to start his syndicated column about the English language with this humorous pronouncement: "The Court of Peeves, Crotchets & Irks opens its assizes with a motion from . . ."

autodidact a self-taught individual
(AW-tō-DĪ-dakt)

No apples for the teacher here—I can learn it myself, thank you, says the autodidact.

Some musicians are autodidacts, teaching themselves to read music.

bereft deprived, desolate (bi-REFT)

One could say *bereaved* and mean the same thing as *bereft*, but why deprive ourselves of the lovely, lonely, keening sound of this word for "loss"?

His absence was keenly felt, leaving them bereft of hope.

bespoke customized (bi-SPŌK)

There's *made-to-order* and *custom-made*, and then there's that so-very-Bond-Street way to say it. Raise one eyebrow as you utter it.

Part of the appeal of Starbucks is bespoke coffee, made the way each customer likes it.

callipygian possessing an attractive posterior (kal-uh-PIJ-ee-un)

Today we might say, "Nice ass, Aphrodite," but the Greeks gave their gorgeous goddess's attribute one of their famously long words—*kallipygos*—which suggests beauty and buns.

Viewed from behind, _____ is callipygian. (Fill in the name of your choice.)

canon a group of standards or principles (KAN-un)

Canon and *cane* are kissing cousins. Both have their origins in the idea of a measuring rod.

The canons of polite society dictate what one can and cannot do.

concordance the principal words in a text
(kun-KOR-dunss)

Such an alphabetical listing, with citations of each passage in which the word appears, used to be the province of Shakespearean scholars and other smarties. Now we can all know it—it's one of Amazon's book features.

A Shakespearean concordance can cite all of the passages that contain "wherefore."

conundrum a puzzle (kuh-NUN-drum)

It's puzzling as to how this word got its start, but perhaps the answer can be found in a pun, which is what a conundrum's answer often is.

Here's a conundrum from word maven Richard Lederer: "What's the favorite food of mathematicians? Pumpkin pi."

derring-do bold activity (DE-reen-DOO)

Be daring and use this term, which harks back to Middle English (although it was not originally intended as a noun). Then dare those who haven't read this book to try to correct your *derring* to *daring*.

Kids on skateboards exhibit derring-do as they perform potentially dangerous moves.

doggerel trivial verse (DOG-er-ull)

Among professional poets, doggerel dogs. What would you expect from a word that literally means "worthless"?

Even Abraham Lincoln was not above writing
doggerel, although today the originals of these
throwaway ditties are worth a bundle.

eleemosynary depending on charity
(ell-ee-uh-MAH-sin-ar-ee)
> Granted, the word *begging* gets you to about the
> same place as this mouthful, but *eleemosynary* is
> a more charitable way of saying it.

In Tennessee Williams's A Streetcar Named Desire,
Blanche DuBois was eleemosynary: she always
depended on the kindness of strangers.

elide to omit (i-LĪD)
> Think *slide* and you get a sense of how slick
> *elide* is, dropping a vowel here and a syllable
> there in pronunciation, or conveniently ignoring
> a fact.

Because synonymous words mean roughly the same
thing, their subtle differences are sometimes elided.

epigraph an inscription (EP-i-graf)
> If it sounds too much like *epitaph*, remember
> that an *epigraph* may be set in stone, but not on
> a tombstone.

Many books include epigraphs, or quotations, at the
beginning. Pablo Medina's The Cigar Roller *carries*
this one from Wallace Stevens: "The imperfect is our
paradise."

eponymous of the same name (i-PON-uh-mus)
> What's in a name? *Eponymous*, that's what, and the name of this game is for the name to be the same—like so:

Vera Wang *and* Ralph Lauren *are eponymous for the names of the people who created these fashion labels.*

equipollent equivalent (ek-wuh-POL-unt)
> *Equivalent* has met its equal in *equipollent*, a word that indicates when two or more of something are equally effective.

Although there are an abundance of sunscreen products, many of them are equipollent in their ability to block the sun's harmful rays.

foil a strong contrast (FOYL)
> *Foil* is a foil for long-winded explanations. It's an economical way to say what would take far longer without the word. When used as a noun, a foil is a person or thing that serves as a contrast to another and helps place the other in a positive light. It's your good cop/bad cop.

Dr. Watson served as a foil for Sherlock Holmes, often bumbling and dithering while Holmes zeroed in on who the killer was.

fortnight two weeks (FORT-nīt)
> The British are fond of *fortnight*. It's shorter than saying "fourteen nights," which is what it means.

Alexis de Tocqueville (1805–1859) spent two weeks

on the American frontier, and the English translation of his account is called A Fortnight in the Wilderness.

huzzah hurrah (huh-ZAH)

Where will you ever say *huzzah*, you're wondering. Try the yacht club. Sailors hoisting sails and heaving ho are most likely the source. The double *z* gives it zip.

As the Tall Ships sailed into port, the crowd shouted huzzahs of appreciation.

inkhorn pedantic (EENK-horn)

You hear the term (if you hear it at all) in relation to inkhorn words, meaning those obscure words that nobody uses anymore. *Inkhorn* is teetering on being one of them. Some inkhorn trivia for you: in its literal sense, an inkhorn was a container made of horn that held ink. To "smell of the ink-horn" was to sound pedantic.

Robert Cawdrey, the compiler of the first English dictionary (1604), was not a fan of inkhorn terms, but his dictionary still had some of these unfamiliar and essentially unusable words. Obnubilate, *anyone?*

malaprop a contusion of similar-sounding words (MAL-uh-prop)

Oops! Make that a *confusion* of similar-sounding words. This kind of verbal mangling is just what Mrs. Malaprop, the only memorable character from a long-forgotten eighteenth-century play, excelled at. The wordsmith Willard Espy shared some of his favorite malapropisms in his last *Words at Play* almanac: "statue of lamentations... erroneous zones... relapse and enjoy it."

"Explain to me in words of one cylinder" is one of the many malapropisms an early radio personality, Jane Ace, uttered. Sorry, Jane, malaprop needs at least three cylinders to explain.

masque a play in which the performers wear masks (MASK)

These masked plays are a throwback to the seventeenth century, although on a metaphoric level, some of us think they're still being performed on Capitol Hill.

At the masquerade ball, guests were invited to be part of an impromptu masque, with the play's characters based on their masks.

mondegreen misheard words (MON-di-green)

Lady Mondegreen, meet Richard Stands. You're both words misheard. Lady Mondegreen is from a folk song whose lyrics were really, "They had slain the Earl of Murray / And *laid him on the green*." Richard Stands is familiar to many youngsters learning the Pledge of Allegiance: "...and to the Republic *for which it stands*..."

Since mondegreens are words misheard rather than misread, a good way to avoid them is to read the song, poem, or other piece you're listening to.

palimpsest paper repeatedly written on and erased (PAL-imp-sest)

> That's the prosaic way to define *palimpsest*. On a philosophical level, what we're really talking about is reinvention, and how you can keep rewriting your life story. Just remember, though, that palimpsests don't have perfect, clean erasures, so a little bit of what used to be there will always remain.

Gore Vidal titled his memoir Palimpsest, *thus letting the reader know he was still (re)writing the final chapters.*

penultimate next to the last (pen-UL-tuh-mit)

> If you're very, very British, you can get away with shortening it to *penult*, and you'll no doubt have the last word.

Y *is the penultimate letter of the alphabet, just one before the last letter,* Z.

penumbra almost a shadow (pe-NUM-bruh)

> Haul this word out for the next eclipse—that's when there's likely to be just such a gray area near the sun or moon. It's a bit like the shady side of the street on a sunny day. Used metaphorically, *penumbra* can shine.

A penumbra of melancholy surrounded her happiness, making it all the more poignant.

petard a small explosive device (pi-TARD)

> Put another way: a petard is something not to

be hoisted with. Why? Because the origin of the word means "to break wind." 'Nuff said? From there it morphed to mean a small bomb of the sort that could blast through a fortification. But the reason this word is useful is that you can now bandy about the phrase "hoist with one's own petard," which means to be caught in your own trap.

Having been hoist with his own petard, he had no desire to shoot himself in the foot a second time.

portmanteau one word that's a blend of two (port-man-TŌ)

Examples of portmanteau words include *smog* (*smoke* + *fog*), *brunch* (*breakfast* + *lunch*), and *chortle* (*chuckle* + *snort*). This last was a favorite of Lewis Carroll, who was the first to apply the meaning of *portmanteau* (literally, "a suitcase with two compartments") to words.

In his blog, author Steve Leveen has coined the word boovies, *a portmanteau of "books" and "movies."*

rebus a pictorial representation of a word or phrase (REE-bus)

If that sounds puzzling, it is—literally. Rebuses are often word riddles, games in which objects represent words.

Picture several bridal veils and the top of a head, and you have a rebus for the first word of the title of Evelyn Waugh's novel, Brideshead Revisited.

semiotics semantics (see-mee-OT-iks)

Semiotics focuses on the meaning of words, whereas phonetics focuses on their sound.

Semiotics and short skirts have something in common: just as with hemlines, certain meanings of words fall in and out of fashion.

spoonerism a transposition of initial letters in adjacent words (SPOO-nur-iz-um)

A little huddle stops the curt. There: you've just been spoonered, and it's not to be confused with being spooned. *A little cuddle stops the hurt* un-spooners the sentence. This delightful linguistic mix-up is named after Spilliam Wooner—make that William Spooner (1844–1930).

See if you can unravel this famous spoonerism that Spooner, who taught at Oxford, reportedly said to a student: "You have hissed all your mystery lectures and tasted two whole worms."

suzerain an overlord (SOO-zuh-rin)

A not-so-distant cousin of *sovereign*, and with the same sense of a ruler or state that lords over others.

Some coaches act like suzerains, treating their players like subjects who owe them blind fealty.

trope a word used figuratively (TRŌP)

Trope comes from the Greek for "turn," and a turn of a phrase is a trope, from a literal to a figurative meaning. (See *palimpsest* and *penumbra* on page 89 for some tropes.) A metaphor is a trope.

Instead of saying, "Whenever you mentioned his name, she smiled," try saying it with a trope:
"Whenever you mentioned his name, sunshine broke through on her face."

wherefore why (WAR-for)

Why know *wherefore* when there's *why*? Because it's the easiest way to sound like a Shakespearean understudy. And if for no other reason than to know what Juliet was really asking when she posed that question to Romeo. (It wasn't because she was wondering where he was.)

O Romeo, Romeo, wherefore art thou Romeo?
—Shakespeare, *Romeo and Juliet*

zeugma a rhetorical device that applies one word in two different senses (ZOOG-muh)

Say what? A zeugma does better in motion than in definition. "She bought the ring and his line about its possessing magical powers" uses *bought* in two different senses. "He stole a glance at her and then her watch" uses *stole* in two different senses. A zeugma, like life, is delightfully incongruous.

Spot the zeugma in this sentence: "They watched the clock and the world go by."

8

Picture This

Descriptions that sing, dance,
and act up a little

Adjectives sometimes get a bad rap as being unnecessary words. But these adjectives add impact because of the vivid pictures they paint.

abstruse difficult to understand (ab-STROOSS)
Think of this esoteric word in terms of "concealed," which is where its present meaning got its start.
Her thinking can be so abstruse that it's difficult to know what she's talking about.

acerbic bitter or harsh (uh-SUR-bik)
Bitter is the taste that *acerbic* may leave in your mouth, as its origins are more than Kevin Bacon–close to *acidic*.
His wit is as acerbic as a sour lemon.

assiduous persistent, diligent (uh-SID-yoo-us)
Ironically, this industrious word has its roots in the Latin for "to sit," but it's too attentive to ever lie down on the job.

The devoted little dog is assiduous about sitting at its master's feet.

august majestic (uh-GUST)
Awesome all grown up.
The august formality of the ceremony was enough to inspire awe.

avuncular benevolent (uh-VUNGK-yoo-ler)
Put all the traits of your favorite uncle into this word and there you have it.
His avuncular tone, sympathetic and kind, made it easy for her to take his advice.

beleaguered besieged (bi-LEE-gerd)
You don't need to be in the army to feel as though you're surrounded, engulfed, encompassed, or beleaguered. You could just be in over your head.
The new physician was beleaguered by enormous loans after finishing years of medical training.

bemused confused (bi-MYOOZD)
Confused can happen to anyone. *Bemused* suggests you're bewildered because you're lost in thought. So remember: you're not confused, you're bemused.
Lost in thought as he walked, he looked utterly bemused when he came to the edge of the cliff.

bumptious pushy (BUMP-shuss)
How presumptuous of *bumptious* to think it's the

most important word on the planet—it needs to be bumped down a peg or two.

The bumptious brute bullied ahead of me in line.

callow immature (KAL-ō)

It's ironic that the origin of this word takes us back to *bald*, and to young birds without feathers (that is, bald). By the time most men are bald, they're no longer callow.

His callow behavior was evident in the way he gunned the engine and squealed the tires just driving to the grocery store.

capricious unpredictable (kuh-PREE-shus)

Erratic in a *Breakfast at Tiffany's*, Holly Golightly kind of way.

She acts on a whim, but such capricious behavior is part of her charm.

chastened subdued (CHĀ-sind)

Find someone *chastened* and there has often been some kind of *castigating*, so it's no surprise the two words are cut from the same etymological cloth.

After getting a thorough scolding, the chastened child sat quietly at the table.

circumspect discreet (SUR-kum-spekt)

There's not a rash bone in this word's body. A cautious word, it keeps its own counsel.

Some people say whatever comes to mind; others are more circumspect.

conciliatory appeasing (kun-SIL-ee-uh-tor-ee)

A kiss-and-make-up word that wants more than anything to please and placate.

"It was silly for us to fight," she said, in her best conciliatory voice. "Let's meet each other halfway."

diffident reserved (DIFF-i-dent)

Here's why you don't want to be diffident: it suggests you mistrust yourself. Don't be diffident—believe!

Her diffident smile was a sign of her shyness.

dilatory delaying, tardy (DIL-uh-tor-ee)

We'll get around to telling you more about this word after we're through procrastinating—which is what dilatory types excel at.

He reveled in being dilatory, putting off till tomorrow what he could have done yesterday.

effete decadent (i-FEET)

Rhymes with *deplete*, and those who are decadent are often depleted of energy (among other things). Put your nose in the air when you meet *effete*, as the word is often coupled with *snob*.

His overly refined, indulgent lifestyle made him an effete snob.

erudite scholarly (AR-yuh-dīt)

Use this word and you'll sound like what it suggests: learned and smart.

Some erudite thinkers write such scholarly tomes that only the equally learned can understand them.

estimable esteemed (ESS-tuh-muh-bull)
   Estimable is admirable, so don't underestimate its power to please.
The estimable David McCullough has many admirers of his books on American history.

fatuous foolish (FACH-oo-us)
   A good alternative when you've run the gamut of *dumb*, *stupid*, and *what were you thinking*.
His infatuation with her was so intense, he found himself doing fatuous things around her and later wondering why he'd been such a fool.

formidable fearsome (FOR-mi-duh-bull)
   When a feeling of dread comes over you, there's probably a formidable person or thing behind it.
A funnel cloud is a formidable sign that a tornado is approaching.

fractious irritable (FRAK-shuss)
   Cranky, peevish, quarrelsome, cross—just thinking about *fractious* makes us so.
His detractors said John Adams was fractious because he was so often argumentative.

fulsome excessive and offensive (FULL-sum)
   It's fitting that the word is rooted in *well fed*,

which suggests full. Often fulsome behavior belongs to someone who's full of it.

His fulsome praise was more infuriating than had he said nothing.

grotesque bizarre (grō-TESK)

"Grotty," say the Brits, and the slang is just a vowel off from *grotesque*'s bizarre beginning in *grotto*, a cave where monstrous-looking creatures were often painted. Nero, the monstrous Roman dictator, liked that style of art—which seems natural, given his cavemanlike lack of refinement.

The sci-fi flick showed humans turning into werewolves, their faces distorted in a grotesque transformation.

hirsute hairy (hur-SOOT)

Just a more diplomatic and refined way to say it.

"He was handsome and hirsute, and she longed to run her hand through his thick hair." (Opening sentence of a badly written bodice ripper.)

histrionic overly dramatic (hiss-tree-ON-ik)

You don't have to be an actor to be emotional in the extreme, but it helps, since *histrionic* takes its cue from the original word for "actor."

Her exaggerated movements and overwrought tone were histrionic enough to command the attention she craved.

hoary ancient (HOR-ee)

> *Hoary* shares an etymological bunk with *gray*, and *gray*—as in beards and hair—is often paired with *ancient*.

In the Arthurian legend, Merlin is usually depicted as a hoary wizard, his hair and beard gray with age.

inane foolish (i-NĀN)

> You could say "of all the dumb-ass . . ." or you could say *inane* instead. It all depends on whom you're saying it to.

Of all the inane things to do, why would you wear shoes in the swimming pool?

inimical hostile (i-NIM-ik-ul)

> Change those first two *i*'s to *e*'s, and you start to see an enemy in *inimical*.

America and Russia no longer have the inimical relationship they had during the Cold War. They claim they're now friends.

insipid dull (in-SIP-id)

> A lively way to say *boring, uninteresting, tasteless, vapid*. At least the words that mean "dull" aren't.

His character in the play was insipid, not an interesting bone in his body, and bordered on lifeless.

intractable unmanageable (in-TRAK-tuh-bull)

> A bad hair day by another name: *stubborn, unruly, obstinate, hard to work with*.

Some actors who become stars also become intractable, making them difficult to work with.

lissome supple (LISS-um)

Jack be nimble, Jack be limber, Jack be lithe and lissome. Who wouldn't want to be Jack?

She credited yoga for keeping her body lissome, since it kept her joints flexible.

lugubrious gloomy (loo-GOO-bree-us)

Deep in its mournful depths, there's a hint of the drama queen in *lugubrious*. Its exaggerated sadness is like sorrow on steroids.

The lugubrious look on his face was ludicrous. How could he be that sad about stepping on an ant?

obstreperous boisterous (ub-STREP-ur-us)

Emerson perhaps characterized it best when he said: "Obstreperous roarings of the throat," since the word means "loud and unruly"—and with a lusty, let-'er-rip sound to it.

They were obstreperous in the extreme, partying loudly into the night.

opaque obscure (ō-PĀK)

Obscure is in itself a somewhat obscure meaning of *opaque*, but it's not too much of a leap from *opaque*'s more common meaning of "not transparent." Summon it when you need a tactful way to describe someone who's difficult to understand or connect with.

*His reasoning was opaque, and because it wasn't
clear, the rest of us had a hard time following it.*

percipient perceptive (pur-SIP-ee-unt)

If you quickly grasped that *perceive* was the etymological engine behind *percipient*, then you are
just such a quick study.

*He was by nature percipient, able to quickly
comprehend the subtlety of a situation.*

perspicacious astute (per-spi-KĀ-shus)

We bet you can count on one hand the number
of times you've actually heard someone say this
word for *shrewd*, *keen-eyed*, or *discerning*. Some
words are better read than said.

*A perspicacious observer sees more than a mere smile
on Mona Lisa's face.*

profligate dissolute (PROF-luh-git)

Not what you want to be if you're trying to
score Brownie points with the Girl Scouts. It
means you're *dissipated, wasteful, of low moral
character*—basically, a mess.

*Nightlife in Las Vegas can easily reflect profligate
behavior, with money and morals freely abandoned.*

prosaic dull (prō-ZĀ-ik)

If you find much of today's prose boring, this
might perk you up: *prosaic* is where the word
prose comes from.

His poetry was eloquent, but his prose was prosaic.

puckish impish (PUK-ish)

A mischievous sprite named Puck had a part in Shakespeare's *Midsummer Night's Dream*, and he's still the imp of choice.

The little boy's puckish grin told his mother he was up to mischief.

pugilistic related to fist fighting (pyoo-juh-LISS-tik)

Put up your dukes, because this is a fighting word, hand-to-hand, *mano a mano*.

It was an old-fashioned pugilistic fight, but what was not so old-fashioned was seeing two women in the boxing ring.

pusillanimous cowardly (pyoo-suh-LAN-i-muss)

"Scaredy-cat" is totally appropriate here, as the Latin derivative of this word indicates the weak young of an animal.

The Cowardly Lion in The Wizard of Oz *was, indeed, a pusillanimous creature.*

rapacious extraordinarily greedy (ruh-PĀ-shus)

So greedy that you'll seize whatever you can (*seize* is the word's root). If rapacious is what you are, plunder is what you do.

Gift cards in hand, they stormed the department store like rapacious marauders, seizing every good buy in sight.

recondite deep, profound (REK-un-dīt)

What you might call people who are so smart you don't have a clue what they're saying. But this word will make you sound as if you do.

I reckon I didn't understand a word that recondite speaker said.

redoubtable formidable (ri-DOWT-uh-bull)

Remember that high school teacher you were scared of but not really? More like someone powerful that you really respected? That teacher was redoubtable.

The redoubtable opera star held the audience spellbound as she held (and held) the note.

sententious pompously pithy (sen-TEN-shus)

Those who are sententious come off as self-righteous, moralizing with maxims and other trite sayings.

She spoke little and, when she did, was sententious, uttering such aphorisms as "No use crying over spilt milk."

snarky cranky (SNAHR-kee)

If *snarky* is *cranky*, does that make a *snark* a *crank*? Actually, no. The two words are apples and artichokes. *Snark* is the fanciful creature (and word) that Lewis Carroll created in his 1876 work, *The Hunting of the Snark*. Jack London later used the word in recounting his South Seas adventures in *The Cruise of the Snark*.

He was irritable and short-tempered, and his mood
was evident in his snarky comments about the movie.

supercilious contemptuous (soo-per-SIL-ee-us)
    This implies a curled-lip case of feeling superior
    to the rest of the world.
The cat appeared to have a supercilious sneer on its
face as it leapt onto the roof and out of reach.

taciturn untalkative (TASS-i-tern)
    Not only has the cat got your tongue but it's not
    about to let go. Ever.
The taciturn husband appreciated the social ease of
his talkative wife.

trenchant incisive, vigorous (TREN-chunt)
    Trenchant types are not warm and fuzzy. They
    tend to have sharp edges and to be a bit cutting.
    And *cutting* is at the root of this word.
The company had a trenchant policy about drugs
and alcohol: it would tolerate neither.

trepid fearful (TRE-pid)
    These days, if you say you're anxious, it's not
    clear whether you're apprehensive or eager. Say
    you're trepid and they'll know you're apprehen-
    sive.
The thought of the interview made him so trepid,
he trembled.

unctuous insincerely earnest (UNK-choo-us)
Think gunk-tuous, as in slimy and slippery.
He was always trying to butter her up, and his
unctuous manner betrayed his empty flattery.

vapid lacking interest (VAP-id)
Dull, but a more interesting way to say it.
The vapid conversation needed to be livened up, so I
told a funny story.

venerable worthy of respect (VEN-ur-uh-bull)
A case when hero worship is called for, because
the person or thing that's venerable is old, wise,
or otherwise dignified.
The venerable Queen Elizabeth 2 *ocean liner is a*
storied tradition in the annals of transatlantic
crossings.

wanton arrogantly reckless (WAHN-tun)
If it's scruples you're seeking, you'll find *wanton*
wanting. *Wanton* goes its willful way, with no re-
gard for right or wrong.
It was a wanton attack on his character, unprovoked
and uncalled for.

9

Sounding Off

Music to the ears

Remember *onomatopoeia*? It's a term many of us learned in school, and it describes words that sound like their meaning (think of *buzz*). You'll find some of them in this chapter.

bombilating humming or buzzing
(BUM-bil-ā-teen)

You don't hear this word much anymore—perhaps the world has become too noisy—but you'll hear Dylan Thomas say it every time you read *A Child's Christmas in Wales*. Mrs. Prothero shouts "Fire!" and rings the dinner gong:

. . . and the gong was bombilating, and Mrs. Prothero was announcing ruin like a town crier in Pompeii.
—Dylan Thomas

celerity swiftness (se-LE-ri-tee)

Learn this word with alacrity—in other words, be quick about it.

"Action This Day" was a small printed tag that Winston Churchill attached to urgent memoranda during World War II. It was a way, says the Churchill Centre, "to encourage celerity on the part of his correspondents."

coda conclusion (KŌ-duh)

You could say "tail end" and mean the same thing, but why not hark back to *tail*'s tail and use this Latin derivative instead?

If a symphony bores you, hearing the coda will console you: it's almost over.

coloratura a musical trill (kul-er-uh-TOOR-uh)

The high-octave equivalent of adding a little color to the cheeks, tra-la.

The operatic soprano Beverly Sills knew how to use coloratura to make a plain note sing.

desuetude disuse (DESS-wi-tood)

The French have a way of making even the negative sound nice. The level of disuse suggested here borders on neglect. Don't let this refined word for it suffer from desuetude. Use it when you can.

Portable CD players have fallen into desuetude since the advent of the MP3 player.

elegiac sorrowful (el-uh-JĪ-uk)

Don't mourn too much for this graceful word. Though sad in meaning, it's sibilant in sound.

Her lyrics possessed an elegiac tone that whispered mournfully in your ear.

elixir a cure-all (i-LIX-ur)
> Such a potent potion is *elixir*—it's the secret to long life. If only it were real.

Some say love is an elixir, the panacea for all that ails us. Others swear by chocolate.

euphonious harmonious (yoo-FŌ-nee-us)
> *Euphonious* is a bit like *euphoria*. Something euphonious makes you feel good because it sounds good.

The euphonious call of the foghorn at Point Judith Light welcomes the fishermen returning home to Rhode Island.

frisson excited shudder (free-SŌN)
> It rhymes (almost) with "bring it on": a shiver or tingle, usually of the desirable sort.

Seeing the pastry cart sent a frisson of pleasure through her sweet tooth.

leitmotif a recurring theme (LĪT-mō-teef)
> *Leit* is German for "to lead," and *leitmotifs* are leaders of the pack. They are the music, slogans, or graphics that dominate a song, campaign, or presentation.

"The New Frontier" was the leitmotif of the Kennedy administration.

mellifluous smooth (muh-LIFF-loo-us)

Sweet as honey is this mellow-sounding word, and *honey* is where *mellifluous* gets its etymological start. Just go with its flow.

Her silky voice had a mellifluous quality to it.

plenitude abundance (PLEN-i-tood)

Plenitude = "plenty," poetically said.

The vineyard was full, with a plenitude of grapes calling to be harvested.

sprezzatura the difficult made to look easy (spretz-uh-TOOR-uh)

Think of the hearty Italian way of saying "That's *amore*," and say *sprezzatura* with as much gusto. A true Italian would make it look (and sound) easy.

The way a professional ice skater performs the difficult triple jumps is a feat of sprezzatura.

synesthesia when a stimulus for one sense also triggers another sense (sin-esth-EE-zhuh)

A sort of sensory two-for-one sale, in which two different sensations arise from one stimulus. You hear music and you see certain colors. You see colors and you visualize certain letters. Not everyone gets this double dose of stimulation, so enjoy it if you do.

Some who study synesthesia believe the painter Kandinsky saw certain colors when he listened to music.

titillate to excite (TIT-uh-lāt)

> If *titillate* tickles your fancy, it's because the Latin root means "tickle." *Titillate* is always topped off with a tingle of pleasure.

His touch still titillated after all these years.

undulating wavy (UN-joo-lā-teen)

> The rhythmic cadence of *undulating* is like the quality it describes.

When you live by the sea, the undulating ebb and flow of the tide set a rhythm to the day.

verisimilitude truth (var-i-suh-MIL-i-tood)

> How could a word this long be anything but the truth? It started off as *verum*, or "truth," and just kept adding more. Honest.

The so-called reality shows are testing the boundaries of verisimilitude, and audiences are becoming skeptical.

10

Sense and Sensuousness

Say it with feeling with these evocative words

These words either suggest the sensual or simply sound sensual.

besotted stupefied (bi-SAHT-ed)
Whenever you're tempted to say that someone's acting like a crazy fool (*fool* being this word's root), say *besotted* instead, and it will slightly cushion the blow.
My dear, you are so besotted with drink, it's time we put the bottle away.

carnal sexual (KAHR-null)
Technically it also means "worldly, temporal, and sensual," but *carnal* usually gets right to the point about getting physical.
The movie Carnal Knowledge *was notorious for its sexual content.*

oenophile a wine lover (EN-ō-fīl)
Bacchus would be raising his Greek drinking cup to salute those who love (*phile*) his wine (*oeno*).

Filled with beautiful wineries, Napa Valley is an oenophile's paradise.

olio a potpourri (Ō-lee-ō)

Lots of cooks are stirring this proverbial pot, and the Spanish *olla*, or "pot," is how this term for a hodgepodge or medley got cooked up in the first place.

The kitchen design was an olio of different colors and textures.

oysterwench a low woman (OY-stur-wench)

That definition comes from Dr. Johnson's famous *Dictionary* of 1755. It has to do with that business about oysters being aphrodisiacs. The women who sold them were often selling something else as well.

A sure way to insult an eighteenth-century gentlewoman was to call her an oysterwench. Not advisable for twenty-first-century women either.

quaff to drink with gusto (KWOFF)

You might drink water mixed with Alka-Seltzer, but it's doubtful you'd quaff it. That would be reserved for the five beers you downed so heartily with dinner.

They lifted their mugs in a toast, then quaffed their ale in a few thirsty gulps.

redolent suggestive (RED-l-ent)

Those with a keen sense of smell may eventually

sniff out this word, as it harks back to the word
smell, and often suggests a particular scent.
The garden was redolent of gardenias, reminding her
of the corsage her mother had worn on her wedding
day.

sybaritic luxurious (sib-uh-RIT-ik)
Make that luxurious with a capital *S*. The word
got its start from Sybaris, an ancient Greek city
known for being a tad over the top in the pamper-
me department.
A stay at a grand hotel is a sybaritic experience, with
the staff indulging the guests' every whim.

torrid extremely hot (TOR-id)
The kind of love affair you should have at least
once: a scorcher that leaves you thirsting for
more. Oh yes—it can also describe the weather.
In the movie Body Heat, *the characters carry on a*
torrid love affair that's as hot as the summer when
they meet.

vernissage a private showing (var-ni-SAZH)
A kind of dry run, but more elegantly stated.
Painters often used the day before the opening
of their art exhibition to give their paintings a
final spit and polish. Only it's called *varnishing*,
which is the source of *vernissage*.
They were invited to the vernissage of the museum's
new exhibit and looked forward to seeing the
paintings before everyone else.

visceral intuitive (VISS-er-ul)

"Gut-level," but more tastefully said. (In anatomy, the viscera are the intestines.)

In Blink, *Malcolm Gladwell shows the value of reacting to situations on a visceral level, without overanalyzing them.*

voluptuary a sensualist (vuh-LUP-choo-ar-ee)

Who needs thought-provoking? Darling, this is about feeling good all over. Pass the bonbons and ring for the masseuse.

A spa is a voluptuary's answered prayers, a place to be coddled and pampered.

11

Geography
Lessons

**Get some mileage out of these
expressions that got their
start in a place or space**

Explore these intriguing ways to define where you are, both literally (*abaft*) and figuratively (*Rubicon*).

abaft behind (uh-BAFT)
If you sit in a back row of the plane, you're sitting abaft, or astern: toward the rear. Although the word is a nautical term, the airplane example is appropriate, as pilots often borrow terms from their nautical cousins.
To guarantee that no one will sit behind you on the flight, sit abaft of everyone else.

ambit circuit, scope, or bounds (AM-bit)
To wrap your brain around this word, think *around*, as in *surround* and in *ambient* (*ambit's* close cousin).
The ambit of their devotion to each other knew no bounds.

Augean stable dirty in the extreme
(aw-JEE-un STĀ-bull)

The mythological Greek king Augeas, who caused the original mess, had thousands of oxen in a stable he hadn't cleaned for thirty years. They finally had to call in Hercules to tidy it up.

It will take a Herculean effort to clean up this Augean stable of a room.

bailiwick area of expertise (BĀ-luh-wik)

Bailiwick is once removed from *bailiff,* "one who holds jurisdiction," and more than once removed from *town* or *hamlet,* where such jurisdiction might take place. Don't use it on your résumé, but toss it around during the job interview.

Hamlet's bailiwick was spouting soliloquies.

bordello brothel (bor-DEL-ō)

Bordello is more to the point than *house of ill re-pute,* but not as blunt as *whorehouse.*

In Gone With the Wind, *Rhett visits the bordello run by the prostitute Belle Watling.*

circuitous indirect (sur-KYOO-i-tus)

A roundabout way of saying just that.

They took a circuitous route to Cape Cod, going round the roundabouts and taking every road but the one that led directly to their destination.

circumscribe to restrict (sur-kum-SKRĪB)

The opposite of "don't fence me in," as that's exactly what *circumscribe* is doing.

Their sphere of influence grew more circumscribed as they traveled in smaller and smaller circles.

donnybrook a free-for-all (DON-ee-bruk)
Tis the Irish we have to thank for this word, which is actually the name of a Dublin 'burb. In centuries past, the annual Donnybrook Fair was infamous for its brawls.
The game ended in a donnybrook, with both sides in an uproar over the outcome.

empyrean the high heavens (em-PEER-ee-un)
No pie in the sky, this *empyrean*: it signals up high, as high as heaven can get.
Once you get beyond earth and reach the empyrean, all we can say is, heaven help you.

firmament the heavens or sky (FUR-muh-munt)
Terra firma isn't the only thing permanent; so is the sky, in the sense of firmament. (Ever see a day without one?)
A few bright stars pierced the blackness of the night firmament.

interstitial pertaining to a narrow opening (in-tur-STISH-ull)
For the Beatles, there was here, there, and everywhere. For *interstitial*, there's here, there, and the small space in between here and there.
The interstitial design of the fence left enough room for the chipmunk to squeeze through the slats.

lyceum a lecture hall (lī-SEE-um)

> Aristotle taught in the first lyceum, although it was not a hall at all but a grove near the temple of Apollo in Athens.

America's nineteenth-century lyceums were the sites of lively discussions about political and social issues.

Pandora's box source of unforeseen problems (pan-DAW-ruhz box)

> Gotta love those Greeks for a good story. This time it's about the first mortal woman, Pandora, who's given a box she's forbidden to open. Of course she does, and out fly the evils of the world. One good thing, however, doesn't escape the chest, and that's hope. We can only.

Attempting to fix the car yourself will open a Pandora's box.

pantheon a temple for the gods (PANTH-ee-on)

> Yes, it's those Romans again, forever building shrines to keep their many gods happy. Today *pantheon* signals hero worship that's been super-sized, and refers to a metaphoric shrine to those mortals we treat like gods.

Babe Ruth and Ted Williams are among the pantheon of baseball greats.

perigee close to earth (PAR-uh-jee)

> At a certain point, the moon is as close as it's going to get to the earth. For moon and earth, that's as good as it gets—that's the perigee.

The fans could get no nearer to their idol than if he were the earth, they were the moon, and their orbit had reached its perigee.

peripatetic walking about (pe-ri-puh-TET-ik)
Aristotle and his boys get credit for this one. In ancient Athens, the *peripatos* was a building with a covered walkway where Aristotle held class for his students.
The peripatetic Thoreau covered much ground, both physical and philosophical, during his long walks.

philistine an uncultured person (FIL-i-steen)
Apparently there are enough such persons because there used to be a place called Philistia. *Philistine* is what someone going to a wine tasting would call someone hitting a keg party.
Highbrows look upon lowbrows as philistines and boors, while lowbrows see highbrows as nothing but bores.

prelapsarian before the fall of humankind
(pree-lap-SAR-ee-un)
Talk about a lapse in judgment: that bit with Adam and the apple really put the kibosh on those prelapsarian days in paradise.
In religious stories, Eden is mainly portrayed in a prelapsarian context. Once Adam and Eve fall from grace, all hell breaks loose.

propinquity proximity (prō-PING-kwi-tee)
Come closer, says *propinquity*, I like you near
and dear. It makes us more alike. It makes us almost kin.
*Their propinquity to one another as kids resulted in
the cousins being close all their lives.*

Rubicon an irreversible step (ROO-bi-kon)
When Julius Caesar crossed the Rubicon River
in Italy, he knowingly started a war that would
be either his undoing or his ultimate victory (it
was the latter). People have been crossing their
own Rubicons, or points of no return, ever since.
*When the political refugees fled the country, they
crossed the Rubicon: there could be no going back.*

serendipity a happy accident (se-run-DIP-i-tee)
Seek and you shall find, but sometimes you find
something good when you're not looking for it.
Horace Walpole coined this word in the eighteenth century, inspired by the constant and unexpected good fortune of *The Three Princes of
Serendip*, a Persian fairy tale. Serendip was an
early name for Ceylon, which is now Sri Lanka.
*Coming upon the huge pink conch shell as they
combed the beach was pure serendipity, since they
were not expecting to find such a beauty.*

ubiquitous omnipresent (yoo-BIK-wit-us)
The only way to be everywhere at once is to be
ubiquitous.

*You're here, I'm there, but that ubiquitous cloud cover
is everywhere.*

via dolorosa a long ordeal
(VEE-uh duh-luh-RŌZ-uh)
> Literally, the "sad road," and one that will not be
> easy to traverse.

*Serious illnesses set both patients and their families on
a via dolorosa.*

watershed a dividing point (WAH-tur-shed)
> Literally, it's what divides two drainage areas.
> Figuratively, it suggests a divide so pronounced
> that it's a turning point.

*The Internet has been a watershed for advertising,
creating a demarcation between old and new media,
and radically changing how messages reach their
audiences.*

12

Spice of Life

Add variety with a compelling
choice of word

These are words that describe something unusual, as *echolalia* and *luthier* do, or words that are an unusual way to describe something, as *animadversion* and *badinage* are.

abeyance suspension (uh-BĀ-unss)

If words were novels, *abeyance* would be *Great Expectations*. It means "temporarily inactive or suppressed," often because you're expecting something, and the Old French word for *expectation* is the root.

You can hold the question of what to serve for dinner in abeyance only so long because your guests will be expecting a meal.

animadversion criticism (an-im-ad-VUR-zhun)

Toss this five-dollar word around the next time people start carping, and your critics may wonder how you got so smart.

He had an aversion to animadversion, preferring praise instead.

attrition gradual wearing down or reduction
(uh-TRISH-un)

>Rooted in the Old French word for "abrasion,"
>*attrition* can indeed cause friction: just think of
>attrition in the workplace.

*The company will use attrition, not replacing workers
when they retire, to cut its workforce.*

audacity daring, adventurousness
(aw-DASS-uh-tee)

>This spirited word was born bold—*bold*, in fact,
>being its Latin root. Use this intrepid adventurer
>of a word as another way of evoking fearlessness.

*"Audacity is the only ticket," wrote Winston Churchill,
who fearlessly took up painting in his forties.*

badinage banter (BAD-n-uzh)

>Surely you jest. And surely *badinage* does, as it's
>rooted in the French word for "jesting and joking."

*Morning talk show hosts engage in badinage when
they want to lighten the mood.*

bombast puffery (BAHM-bast)

>If you've ever been tempted to tell someone
>who was spouting bombast, meaning "pompous
>language," to stuff it, you'd be etymologically
>correct—if not politically so. *Bombast* originally
>referred to cotton wadding used to stuff and
>puff Elizabethan garments.

*He puffed out his cheeks and puffed up his chest and
uttered bombast that was similarly hollow.*

caboodle a collection or crowd
(kuh-BOO-dull)
> Of course, it needs its kit, much like Forrest Gump's carrots need their peas. "The whole kit and caboodle" says "a bunch" with more authority.

In an essay for the New Yorker, *the estimable E. B. White wrote about the state of his brain, or noodle, at that moment:*

Observe, quick friend, this quiet noodle,
This kit removed from its caboodle.
Here sits a brain at last unhinged,
On which too many thoughts impinged.

crucible a harsh test (KROO-suh-bull)
> There are tests of character and tests of patience; if it's a crucible, it's a test that makes any other look easy.

Losing in the first round of playoffs was a crucible for the soccer team.

echolalia repetition of another's words
(ek-ō-LĀ-lee-uh)
> Do I hear an echo? *(Do I hear an echo?)* A person with echolalia repeats the words he or she has just heard someone else say. *(A person with—* you get the idea.)

Albert Einstein, one of the greatest thinkers of our time, was prone to echolalia. How fitting, given that the world continues to repeat his $E = mc^2$.

emollient a softening agent (i-MOLL-yunt)
> Some things soothe the soul, others the skin, as this smooth-sounding word suggests.

The soothing salve was a welcome emollient to his windburned face.

farrow to produce a litter of pigs (FAR-ō)
> Surprisingly, it was the urbane E. B. White, the author of *Here Is New York*, who brought this barnyard term to our attention. He used it in an essay—and he did, after all, have an affinity for a certain porker named Wilbur.

The mama pig farrowed a healthy batch of piglets and seemed relieved to have her newborns around her.

frippery cheap and showy clothing (FRI-puh-ree)
> "Frivolous finery" is another way to know *frippery*, although once upon a time the word was a respectable name for a shop selling secondhand clothes.

At the consignment shop she found a feather boa, satin slippers, and other frippery for the costume party.

inanition exhaustion (in-uh-NISH-un)
> Running on empty (*emptiness* is its root), and not just in a physical sense. Those who are depleted of fresh ideas also know inanition.

After running a grueling race and losing, the candidate's inanition was so great that he was too tired to speak.

indolence laziness (IN-duh-linss)

Indolent individuals would never bother to find another word for "laziness," as they're too busy being slothful.

It wasn't the traffic that made you late for our appointment; it was sheer indolence.

leviathan something huge (li-VI-i-thin)

Something on a scale that makes humans look like Lilliputians. We're talking majorly big, monstrously huge, of biblical proportion. In fact, there is a story of such a leviathan—a sea monster—in the Bible.

The Airbus A380 jumbo jets are leviathans, some of the largest commercial aircraft ever made.

luthier a violin maker (LOO-tee-ur)

Actually, it's a maker of any stringed instrument, including the lute, which is the word's root.

Stradivarius is perhaps the most famous luthier, and his violins are considered masterpieces.

maquette a mini me (mah-KET)

Think doll-house scale. Maquettes are small models of larger structures.

Some furniture designers have maquettes of their pieces to show customers how they can arrange a room in different ways.

noisome noxious (NOY-sum)

You'd think that by its spot in the dictionary

between *noisiness* and *noisy*, *noisome* would be
another variation on making a racket. Actually,
its meaning is closer to making a stink. It suggests something disagreeable, offensive, or mal-
odorous.

*The noisome nature of the melaleuca trees, which
smell like rotting potatoes when they flower, makes
them undesirable inhabitants of homeowners' yards.*

obeisance a bow or curtsy (ō-BĀ-suns)
Obedient souls know who's the boss, and it ain't
them. Hence the deferential bow to the one
who is.

*Bow down, and your obeisance is a signal that you're
willing to obey.*

offal entrails; garbage (OFF-ul)
Just remember awful offal. It's yucky stuff, on
the order of what a butcher would toss. And
you might toss your cookies if you saw it.

*The garbage was heaped in piles, a mass of offal too
awful to mess with.*

panegyric high praise in public (pan-uh-JĪ-rik)
Don't get too excited about the possibility of a
panegyric, because often the public event is a
person's funeral.

*The eulogy was a panegyric of the first order, with
more good words about the deceased than had ever
been heard when he was alive.*

parlance a manner of speaking (PAR-lunss)

Parlez-vouz a particular parlance? The word is from the French *parler*, "to speak," and is right at home with *parlor*, where conversation was customarily held. *Parlance* refers to a specific kind of conversation, bearing on the idiomatic.

In today's parlance, TMI means "too much information."

pedigree lineage (PED-i-gree)

Dogs and horses aren't the only ones for whom breeding counts. Applied to humans, *pedigree* means not just the family tree but also the traits that can make a person appropriate for a situation.

He possessed the perfect pedigree for a diplomat's life: wealth, discretion, and a closet filled with Brooks Brothers suits.

peregrination wandering (pe-ri-grin-Ā-shun)

We call those not-so-happy *Mayflower* wanderers, who shuttled between England and Holland before hopping across the pond, pilgrims. We might have called them peregrinators. If it were a certain roving bird, we'd call it the peregrine falcon.

With the many challenges of air travel today, it's a wonder that globe-trotters still pursue their peregrinations.

platitude a trite remark (PLAT-i-tood)

A platitude has zero attitude. It's more like a

flatitude (*flat* being its root) because it's a flat, dull remark.

"Have a nice day" is a common platitude.

predilection preference (pred-uh-LEK-shun)

We're partial to this word; in fact, we prefer it to many others.

Most kids love sweets, a predilection that can land them in the dentist's chair.

provenance origin (PRAHV-uh-nunss)

An old word often invoked when referring to old things—that is, antiques—and where they came from.

To accurately assess the value of a nineteenth-century painting, you must know its provenance so that you can prove it's not a forgery.

purview scope or range (PUR-vyoo)

In business, it's all about turf, and *purview* is shorthand for "I'm in charge of this."

All accounting activities were under her purview, giving her full authority over the finance department.

riposte a retort (ri-PŌST)

In fencing, *riposte* describes a quick thrust of the sword, so that tells you how sharp and fast this retort is.

Good comedians often come up with a memorable riposte that ends up being the last laugh.

ruction a loud fight (RUK-shun)

A row that causes a ruckus—that's a ruction.
*The two were always at odds, so whenever they
argued, it would erupt into a ruction.*

semaphore a signal (SEM-uh-for)

This signal uses sight rather than sound, and re-
lies on none of the bells and whistles of the elec-
tronic age. Instead, it uses such simple devices
as flags, flashing lights, and arm movements.
*At railroad crossings, the flashing red lights and
mechanical arms serve as semaphores, warning
motorists that a train is coming.*

sojourn a short stay (SŌ-jurn)

The kind of houseguests you want to invite are
those on a sojourn because they won't hang
around long.
*Our sojourn found us in Paris for two days, London
for one, and Dublin for two, giving us just a glimpse
of each.*

solipsism the theory that the self is the sole
reality (SAHL-ip-siz-m)

In other words: "It's all about me."
*"She practices solipsism" has become our catchphrase
for the most self-centered woman in our club.*

surfeit an excess (SUR-fit)

When too much is too much, even of a good
thing, this excess is a surfeit.

Enough already—I've consumed a surfeit of the
sorbet and can't swallow another spoonful.

talisman a good-luck charm (TAL-iss-mun)
> Talismans are common in primitive societies—
> but then again, that navy blue jacket has always
> brought you good luck, hasn't it?

Her charm bracelet was a collection of talismans that
she wore whenever she took an exam.

tautology redundancy of words
(taw-TAHL-uh-jee)
> If we've said it once, we've said it a thousand
> times: *tautology* is an unnecessary repetition of
> different words to make the same point. Let's
> rephrase that: *tautology* uses words that may
> be different to convey the same idea, over and
> over. Put another way . . .

His many excuses for why he didn't show became a
tautology; he said the same thing in different ways
but never really said why.

temerity brashness (tuh-MAR-i-tee)
> *Temerity* could be "bravery" but for the utter
> recklessness of it. There's a fine line between
> no fear and no brains, and *temerity* crosses it.

Their skydiving acrobatics showed they had tons of
temerity and not an ounce of sense.

totem an emblem or a symbol of a group (TŌ-tum)
> In case you think society has evolved beyond

the tribal faces of the totem pole, think again; we've simply adapted totems to fit on more than poles—such as on clothing, for instance, with designer logos for all to see.

Both coats of arms and totems often feature an animal that symbolizes a particular family.

trajectory the path of something that's moving (truh-JEK-tuh-ree)

If you're tired of being told that such-and-such is not rocket science, throw a curve into that theory with *trajectory*. In its most literal application, it's the curve a projectile rocket takes. But that's not the only time you can use this word. Try it this way, too:

Her career trajectory was taking her higher and higher in broadcast journalism, and she hoped to be an anchor with a major network within the year.

umbrage annoyance (UM-brij)

One of those words that takes rather than gives— you take umbrage, or offense, at something.

When she couldn't find a clerk to ring up her purchase, she took umbrage and took her business elsewhere.

usury an exorbitant interest rate (YOO-zhuh-ree)

If you use a credit card, make sure it's not using you through usury.

Even a small loan can have payment terms that border on usury, so always check the interest rate.

vitriol caustic criticism (VI-tree-all)

Although there is such a thing as constructive criticism, it's destructive when it's *vitriol*.

His vitriol was uncalled for—he could have found a tactful way to point out the problem.

voir dire an examination of a prospective juror or witness (vwahr DEER)

Toss this expression around the next time you're called for jury duty, and you'll sound like the lawyers who are about to start the voir dire process, asking you questions to see if they want you on the jury. Just remember, *voir dire* literally means "to speak the truth."

Part of the attorney's voir dire for this criminal case was to ask potential jurors if they believed in the death penalty.

votary a devout follower (VŌ-tuh-ree)

A votary is devoted to someone or something, and would surely vote for that person or thing if possible. *Vote* and *votary* share the same root, which is *vow*.

Votaries of former president Bill Clinton are such faithful supporters that they'd vote for him a third time if they could.

13

Powerhouses

High-octane descriptions that
make your meaning clear

These words bring a precision to what you really mean to say. *Lapidary* is a way to say "precise" that's made all the more effective because of the word's association with stonecutting.

apocryphal of dubious authorship
(uh-PAHK-ruh-full)
> As far back as biblical times, people wrestled with who really wrote what they were reading, and some versions of the Bible reject certain writings as being apocryphal.

Queen Victoria was said to have imperiously pronounced, "We are not amused." But according to the quote sleuth Ralph Keyes, the anecdote is most likely apocryphal.

arcane obscure (ahr-KĀN)
> Your secret's safe with this word, as it loves to be mysterious.

The existence of the Opus Dei religious organization

was arcane knowledge until The DaVinci Code
made it all but a household term.

axiomatic self-evident (ak-see-uh-MAT-ik)
 An axiomatic statement must be regarded as
 universally true to be worthy of the title, and
 worthy is the root of the word.
For the founding fathers, the rights of life, liberty, and
the pursuit of happiness were axiomatic.

bedizened gaudily dressed (bi-DĪ-zend)
 The word just begs for its sidekick *bedecked*, and
 together the two will be dressed to paint the
 town red.
Playing dress-up can result in little girls bedizened in
big girls' clothes.

cumbersome awkward (KUM-bur-sum)
 You could say *clumsy* or *bulky* or *troublesome*,
 but why not use the word that sounds as un-
 wieldy as what it means?
Trying to fit four people in the backseat of a
two-door car is cumbersome, to say the least.

desultory aimless or random (DESS-ul-tor-ee)
 Are you reading this book from beginning to
 end? You're a methodical reader. Are you jump-
 ing around, flipping pages somewhat aimlessly
 and choosing entries at random? You're a desultory reader.

She cruised through the stack of magazines in
desultory fashion, reading snippets here and bits there.

diurnal daytime or daily (dī-UR-null)
> This word has been around so many days—
> since 1550 or so—it's a wonder it isn't part of
> our daily speech. Its close kin is *journal*, which
> originally indicated a daily record.

The athletes adhered to a rigid diurnal schedule of
exercise and practice, from sunrise till sundown.

dormant inactive (DOR-munt)
> What this word will become if you don't use it.
> And it's no accident that the word *dorm* is part of
> it: both hark back to the Latin *dormire*, "to sleep."

Bears that hibernate lie dormant, but don't let the big
snooze fool you—they eventually wake up.

facile easy (FASS-ul)
> When it's so easy it's effortless, and so effortless
> it borders on superficial, it's facile.

The facilitator made the effort of running a workshop
look facile, although it was very demanding.

gratuitous unnecessary (gruh-TOO-uh-tus)
> A more polite way of saying, "Who asked you?"
> It shares dictionary space with *gratuity*, but
> whereas a gratuity is earned, *gratuitous* is some-
> thing free—as in advice you didn't ask for.

The criticism was gratuitous, unwarranted,
unjustified, and unwelcome.

idiopathic unknown, when speaking of the
causes of a disease (id-ee-ō-PA-thik)
> A smart-sounding way of saying you're clueless,
> often used in the medical field, probably because
> patients have paid too much to hear a doctor
> say, "I don't know."

Despite medical advances, there are still idiopathic
diseases that confound the experts and spur them to
continue research into the causes.

inchoate incipient (in-KŌ-it)
> Just begun, therefore incomplete and rudimen-
> tary.

The painting is in the inchoate stage, with barely a
brushstroke applied to the waiting canvas.

ineffable inexpressible (in-EFF-uh-bull)
> If you think words cannot express, *ineffable* can.
> It expresses the indescribable and unutterable.

Holding their newborn for the first time brings parents
a feeling of ineffable joy.

ineluctable inevitable (in-i-LUK-tuh-bull)
> Don't fight it (the *luctare* embedded in *ineluctable*
> means "to wrestle"): it's unavoidable and in-
> escapable that English would have more than
> one word for "inevitable."

Those still wrestling with whether to have a home
computer must accept the unavoidable truth:
electronics are an ineluctable fact of life today.

inured accustomed to (in-YOORD)

If words came with sound effects, the one for *inured* would be a sigh. If you're inured to it, you're used to it. You don't necessarily like it, but you're resigned to it. Sigh.

People who live in equatorial climates become inured to summer thunderstorms.

lapidary exact and precise (LAP-i-dar-ee)

Those who cut precious stones know all about precision. Their word for their craft—*lapidary*—is so good that the rest of us now use it when talking about anything elegantly concise.

William Faulkner was a marvelous writer, but he was not known for his lapidary prose; his tales are far too complicated.

multifarious diverse (mul-ti-FAR-ee-us)

With a language as diverse as English, it makes sense that there would be more than one way to say "diverse," even if it takes a little longer to say it.

The multifarious blogs being written today cover a wide range of topics and appeal to a broad spectrum of interests.

nascent emerging (NĀ-sunt)

Think of *natal* (as in babies) and you'll know *nascent*. It's just the beginning.

Once upon a time not too long ago, computers were a nascent technology and the Internet was yet to be born.

plangent loud and sad (PLAN-junt)

When it's plangent, you hear it loud and clear, and it's always plaintive.

The bell gonged mournfully, its plangent tone signaling the start of the funeral procession.

plausible believable (PLAWZ-uh-bull)

A round of applause for this word, which was once reserved for only those situations that merited applause. Does that sound plausible? Believe it!

It was a plausible excuse, so the teacher gave her an extra day to turn in her paper.

precipitous steep or abrupt (pri-SIP-i-tus)

Precipice hovers perilously close to *precipitous*. No wonder the word so often signals that someone is on edge.

The staff attributed the boss's precipitous shift in mood to the news that the company's stock had just suffered a precipitous fall.

prostrate lying facedown (PROS-trāt)

All those TV commercials about EDF are not referring to pros*trate* but to the pros*tate*. What a difference one little *r* makes. Think of pros*trate* as straight down and pros*tate* as—well, you'll figure it out.

Flinging themselves onto the playing field with whoops of happiness, the victorious rugby players were prostrate with joy.

putative assumed to be (PYOO-tuh-tiv)
> It may or may not be, but if it's putative, it's commonly thought to be.

He knew he was adopted, and that his putative biological father was living in Depew.

risible relating to laughter (RĪZ-uh-bull)
> If this word were a picture, it would be a smiley face. It means both "laughable" and "prone to laughter." Smile when you see *risible* coming.

His comic behavior was risible, getting a big laugh out of the audience.

salient conspicuous or prominent (SĀL-yunt)
> When it's so obvious it all but jumps out at you, it's *salient*, a word grounded in the idea of leaping.

One of Princess Diana's salient traits was her "shy Di" smile.

sedulous diligent (SEJ-uh-lus)
> The same Latin root that gives us *zealous* gives us *sedulous*, a kind of zealotry minus the fanaticism.

He persevered and stuck with it, and this sedulous approach to his golf game paid off: he shaved two strokes off his handicap.

somnolent soporific (SAHM-nuh-lunt)
> And what's *soporific*? you may ask. Both are snoozers of words—but only literally speaking. They mean "sleepy" or "sleep inducing."

Being somnolent is what every insomniac dreams of.

sonorous resonant (suh-NOR-us)

A sonorous voice is anything but a snore. It's rich and full and deep.

Often the most powerful orators possess sonorous voices, their masterful tones commanding both attention and respect.

specious seemingly correct but actually not (SPEE-shus)

It sounds true, it seems true . . . but it's not. Be suspicious of the specious.

When the project failed, there were lots of specious explanations for it, but the truth was, nobody knew what had actually gone wrong.

supine passive (soo-PĪN)

A supine position finds you flat on your back— not exactly a go-get-'em posture, which is why *supine* can also mean "inactive" or "lethargic."

The yoga session ends with all of us supine, palms facing up, our bodies relaxed.

turgid overblown (TUR-jid)

Turgid is from the Latin word for "swell," as in bloated. When used figuratively, it's often be-cause of someone's swelled head.

His turgid prose was grandiloquently bombastic, but he thought it was swell.

unrequited not reciprocated (un-ree-KWĪ-tid)

Everything's a one-way street with *unrequited*, so don't expect anything in return.

Her love for him was unrequited—he never gave her so much as a glance.

uxorious submissive to your wife (uk-SOR-ee-us)
   A fancy word to describe husbands who are programmed to say, "Yes, dear" automatically.
Her uxorious husband always let her pick the restaurant.

vituperative abusive (vī-TOO-pur-uh-tiv)
   A verbal pummeling is in store from someone who's vituperative—it's a way to beat someone up figuratively.
He was constantly berating her, and his vituperative comments eventually wore her down.

14

Storied Terms

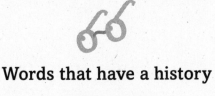

**Words that have a history
and a past**

Most of us love a good story, and words in English are filled with fascinating etymologies. Knowing the story behind the word often helps in remembering—and remembering to use—the word.

aegis protection (EE-jis)
"With your shield or on it" was a favorite saying of the soldiers of antiquity. The aegis was the shield or breastplate of either Zeus or Athena, possibly made from the skin of a goat, which is the root of the word.
Under the aegis of a scholarship, the student is shielded from certain financial obligations.

bellwether leader or leading indicator
(BEL-weh-ther)
Would you believe—we have sheep to thank for this word, as one of the pack has to lead the rest of the bunch. That one out front would be the wether, and it often has a bell around its neck to signal the rest to follow like, well, sheep.

Today's street fashion is often the bellwether of tomorrow's runway fashions.

Bluebeard a wife killer (BLOO-beerd)
This is why a good prenup is so important. Ladies, beware a suitor who calls himself Chevalier Raoul, aka Bluebeard. This seventeenth-century fictitious character had a closetful of dead wives.
If you be a Bluebeard, I be a-looking for someone else to marry.

buccaneer pirate (buk-uh-NEER)
Next time you put a shrimp on the barbie, think of *buccaneer*, as this word got its start with the word *barbecue*. The French pirates of the Caribbean learned how to cook by watching the native islanders barbecue. Those barbecuing pirates became buccaneers.
Hummers are the buccaneers of the highway, ruthlessly claiming the road like pirates about to seize a ship.

canoodle to caress (kuh-NOO-dull)
Don't expect to kiss this word good-bye anytime soon. It may be slang, but it sure knows how to hang, as in "hang around": it's been in use since 1859. Here's how *canoodle* appeared in an 1879 article in England's *Punch* magazine (with a nod to the spelling of the time):

Then he and the Matchless one struggle, snuggle, and
generally conoodle together rapturously.

charette a collaborative design workshop
(shuh-RET)

> How does a word start off meaning "chariot"
> and end up meaning this? It started when French
> architectural students in a design contest would
> literally hop in the *charette*, or wagon (that is,
> *chariot*), to put the final touches on their entries
> as they rolled along the Paris streets to the place
> of competition.

The New Urbanist movement, which fosters
traditional neighborhood design for communities,
holds charettes as a way of soliciting residents'
opinions of the master plan.

draconian harsh (druh-KŌ-nee-un)

> Memo: if a guy named Draco offers you a job,
> give it a miss. He's an ancient Athenian whose
> methods were so harsh, he makes the boss from
> hell look like a cupcake. He's also the reason for
> *draconian*.

The judicial systems of some countries impose
draconian punishments.

emolument a salary or similar compensation
(i-MAHL-yoo-ment)

> From the Latin *emolumentum*, meaning both
> "profit" and "exertion." Even those old Romans
> had to work hard for their money.

His efforts for the company paid off, earning him an
emolument greater than any salary he'd ever
received.

flotsam and jetsam wreckage (FLOT-sum and
JET-sum)

> One is due to a shipwreck (*flotsam*), the other is
> thrown overboard (*jetsam*). Either way, you're
> sunk if you think any of the stuff can be salvaged.

The desk was awash with the flotsam and jetsam of
someone in desperate need of a professional
organizer to sift through the clutter.

galvanize to move to action (GAL-vuh-nīz)

> Imagine trying to get dead frogs to move at all,
> let alone move to action. That's just what the
> Italian physician Luigi Galvani, to whom we owe
> the word's origin, did in the 1700s when he got
> electricity to run through the frogs' legs.

Terrified of slimy creatures, the little girls were
galvanized into running out of the woods and back
to the camp.

gambit a strategic first move (GAM-bit)

> Ever hear the word *gams* for "legs"? *Gambit* got
> its start from the Italian for tripping up your op-
> ponent (by the leg) in wrestling. From there it
> hopped onto the chessboard, where it means
> sacrificing a pawn early on for a later gain. Now
> it means a tactic in other games people play,
> both in business and politics.

The store gambled on its gambit of marking down the merchandise that customers saw first in the hopes that they would buy more.

hackneyed trite (HAK-need)

In the etymological way-back machine, a hackney was a horse for hire. When horsepower replaced horses, the hackney cab became the carriage for hire. (Now we call them taxis.) But it was the writer who would write anything for hire—the hack writer—that led to the meaning of "trite."

"You can lead a horse to water but you can't make him drink" is a hackneyed phrase.

halcyon peaceful (HAL-see-on)

The Romans gave us our word for "happiness," but we can thank the Greeks for taking the idea up a notch with *halcyon.* The Greeks being who they were, there's a story behind it. A kingfisher, its nest floating on the sea and filled with hatchlings, was able to calm the waters into a clear blue tranquillity. *Alkyon* is Greek for "kingfisher."

Whenever I'm stressed out, I think of the halcyon days of that summer at sea, the water tranquil and the breeze soft, and a calming wave washes over me.

harbinger foreshadowing (HAHR-bin-jer)

In the days of Middle English, the *herbeugar* was a kind of advance man, sent on ahead to arrange the hotel stay, or what passed for Marriotts in those days. A *harbinger* continues to be a fore-runner.

Today's erratic weather patterns are a harbinger of the global climate change that the earth is undergoing.

maneuver a shrewd tactic (muh-NOO-ver)

Clever is *maneuver*, but what makes this word even more so is that it shares etymological shelf space with . . . *manure*! It really is true that you could be in deep doo-doo if you mess up on your maneuvers.

The Artful Dodger, the young pickpocket in Oliver Twist, *had many a successful maneuver for filching someone's wallet.*

Manichean dualistic (man-i-KEE-un)

Good and evil, light and darkness: these are the kinds of dualistic elements this philosophy reflects. It was once a popular religion, named for its third-century Persian founder.

They saw the world in terms of us and them, a kind of Manichean approach that left little room for shades of gray.

martinet a rigid disciplinarian (mahr-tin-ET)

Forward . . . march! Traditionally, March is the first month of good weather, so those Romans, forever soldiering on, made it the first month on their calendar. It's a short step from *march* to *martinet*, and many a martinet did the Romans have in their armies. Most of us know a few of these drill sergeants, always ready to give others their marching orders.

The headmaster was a martinet, demanding strict obedience on the part of his students.

maverick a radically independent thinker
(MAV-rik)

Fittingly, we owe the word to one of those independent-minded Texans, Samuel Maverick (1803–1870). He refused to brand his cattle, which came to be called mavericks.

Entrepreneurs are often considered mavericks because their thinking tends to be far outside the box, but their companies frequently become some of the strongest brands.

Occam's razor the simpler answer
(OK-ums RĀ-zur)

Let's cut through the clutter: there's a simpler answer than the complicated one that's out there. Named for a fourteenth-century English philosopher, *Occam's razor* is a variation of the KISS principle. So Keep It Simple, Sweetheart, and don't make any more assumptions than are needed.

"It's the economy, stupid," was the first Clinton campaign's Occam's razor to the country's complicated state of affairs.

paladin a defender (PAL-uh-din)

Paladins were once the palace guard. Now

they're staunch champions of a cause. Don't mess with 'em.

When it comes to consumer protection, Ralph Nader is a legendary paladin.

pariah an outcast (puh-RĪ-uh)

In India, where the caste system is adept at casting out undesirables, the job of beating the drum, or *parai*, at a festival was left to one of the lowlies. A new ploy, perhaps, for getting the kid next door to stop banging on those drums.

High school cliques being what they are, it's easy for one of the less popular kids to feel like a pariah.

philippic a tirade (fi-LIP-ik)

Back in the day, King Philip of Macedon took a lot of verbal abuse from an unsupportive Greek orator. *Philippic* came to mean all that verbal spleen. Today we'd probably witness an unflattering philippic about Phil on YouTube.

As the frenzy of election day nears, the ads of political candidates often degenerate into philippics against one another.

Pyrrhic gain at too great a cost (PEER-ik)

Pyrrhic and *victory* go hand in hand; ironically, they mean a type of failure. Pyrrhus, an ancient Greek king, spent his whole career in combat. He won most battles but tallied staggering losses (including, finally, himself), so his success came at a great price.

It was a Pyrrhic victory, and left them deflated rather than elated.

quisling a traitor (KWIZ-leeng)

The word is the surname of Major Vidkun Quisling, the Norwegian official who collaborated with the Nazis, serving as their puppet when they invaded his country during World War II.

He went from being an embedded spy to being a quisling, betraying his own government.

quixotic overly idealistic (kwik-SAHT-ik)

That romantic, visionary, impractical dreamer Don Quixote is forever with us through this adjective he inspired. There are worse things.

Some see a world that doesn't rely on fossil fuels as nothing but a quixotic quest.

rummage to search through (RUM-ij)

Give us a minute and we'll find the history of this word . . . somewhere. Is it in this stack? No, let's paw through the other one, then riffle through that one, and sift through this one. After all that rummaging, we've found it. At one point the word was *roomage* and indicated a tossing out of stuff in the hold of a ship to make more room.

She rummaged through her handbag, seeing what she might toss out as she tried to make room for the note pad.

scrofula a form of tuberculosis
(SCRAHF-yoo-luh)

Also sometimes called "the king's evil," which is useful to know if you read books set in and around the eighteenth century. The English of that period believed the cure for this malady lay in being touched by the king.

The great lexicographer Samuel Johnson (1709–1784) suffered from scrofula as a child. As is often the case with TB, the disease affected him for the rest of his life.

Sisyphean forever futile (sis-uh-FEE-un)

In Greek mythology, Sisyphus was the poor slob who had to roll the boulder to the top of the hill, only to have it roll down again. So he'd roll it up again and down it would come again. And on and on. Such endless repetition is the stuff that Sisyphean tasks are made of.

Working the assembly line was a Sisyphean task. No sooner did they pull one component off than another one appeared.

Tantalus a tease (TAN-tuh-luss)

Ever known temptation to the point of torment? Talk about yanking somebody's chain: the poor mythological creature who bore this name had to stand in water he could not drink, beneath boughs of fruit he could not reach. This is *tease* with a capital *T*.

The plate of freshly baked cookies was a Tantalus to the toddler, who could not reach the counter where they sat, calling to him.

toady a flatterer (TŌ-dee)

> *Toady* literally means (gulp) "toad eater." It's what the toady would do back in the day of medieval quack medicine. He would swallow a toad while his master (who was masquerading as a doctor) would get a gasping crowd to swallow his line about being a healer. It's questionable whether the toady actually chowed down on the toad— much the way it's questionable whether a modern toady's fawning behavior is sincere.

He's nothing but a toady, so don't swallow his false flattery.

tumbrel the cart of condemnation (TUM-brull)

> In the tumbrel, one takes quite a tumble. First there's the fall from grace that got you into this dump cart in the first place. Then there's the falling off of your head from the guillotine that the tumbrel is carting you off to. The cart that figured so prominently in *A Tale of Two Cities* can create a powerful effect when used figuratively.

As he trundled down the hallway to HR, he felt as if he were in a tumbrel, on his way to getting the ax.

15

What a Surprise

**Use the ordinary in
unordinary ways**

So many of our words have more than one meaning, or more than one way to apply a meaning. Use these words to put a fresh spin on a sentence; they're a sit-up-and-take-notice technique for memorable writing.

acolyte attendant (AK-uh-līt)

Former altar boys know all about being acolytes. It's no sin to use the word in a secular sense as well, for an assistant who serves in a somewhat worshipful way.

It should come as no surprise that in the TV series The Sopranos, *mob boss Tony was blessed with several acolytes.*

anoint to consecrate (uh-NOYNT)

Overlook, for a moment, its messy Latin origins in *smear*, for the holy oil that's often used to anoint someone. This word works in a figurative sense, too.

The CEO anointed his successor without the board's approval, and there was holy hell to pay.

benediction a blessing (ben-uh-DIK-shun)

Try using it the way Mark Twain did so beautifully when he wrote in 1896 of his family's house in Hartford:

To us, our house was not insentient matter—it had a heart, and a soul, and eyes to see us with; and approvals, and solicitudes, and deep sympathies; it was of us, and we were in the peace of its benediction.

chestnut an old, worn-out story (CHESS-nut)

A too-oft-told tale is a chestnut. Another way to think of it: if Uncle Sid tells that Atlantic City Boardwalk story at one more family dinner, you'll go nuts.

"Not that old chestnut!" exclaimed the actor, who was weary of hearing reporters tell the story about his disastrous performance nine years earlier.

chum to lure or bait (CHUM)

Either fish or cut bait—or use some ground-up bait fish to chum for bigger fish. The word works metaphorically as well as for the day's catch.

The reporter was chumming for a bigger story, baiting the senator with loaded questions.

collateral promotional material (kuh-LAT-ur-ul)

A great chameleon word, this. In the military, *collateral* is usually coupled with *damage* to indicate civilians caught in the crossfire. In the finance world, it's what your house is to the lending institution that holds your mortgage. But in the world

of marketing and public relations, *collateral* refers to promotional material, such as a brochure.
Among the bank's collateral is a brochure promoting affordable home ownership.

compact an agreement (KOM-pakt)

Are we all in agreement that this use of *compact* is another way to say "contract" or "covenant"? Good—then it's binding.
The friends had a compact that none would go unless all could go, and they honored this agreement for years.

compass to comprehend (KUM-pus)

Somewhere along the etymological highway, this word veered off course. It used to be common for *compass* to go in two directions, as both a verb and a noun, but now you hear it mostly as a noun. Try it as a verb.
The yacht's crew could not compass why the captain abruptly changed course.

conceit an opinion or idea (kun-SEET)

Sometimes a great notion is known as a conceit. (Other times *conceit* simply indicates a favorable opinion—especially of yourself.)
He carried a small note pad with him, the better to capture his conceits as they came to mind.

epiphany a sudden and significant insight (i-PIF-uh-nee)

The word is often associated with the Christian

feast day of the three kings on January 6, when Christ first appeared to the Gentiles. It's a powerful word, best reserved for important revelations.

Coming to realize that I could, indeed, find my way around a strange city on my own was a welcome epiphany.

gull to trick (GUL)

If you can gull someone into believing it's really the sun that revolves around the earth, you can probably get that person to swallow anything— much as a seagull swallows whatever food you toss it. And no, we're not gulling you about the word's connection to *swallow*.

You can't fool all the people all the time, but you can almost always gull the gullible.

hobble to hamper (HAH-bull)

Although *hobble* is another word for *limp*, it's also a great way to say "impede" (to the point where what's being impeded may start to limp).

High winds hobbled the efforts of the window washers working on the high-rise.

legion numerous (LEE-jun)

The largest unit of the Roman army was the 6,000-man legion. Those fellows are gone now, but *legion* still marches to the beat of meaning multitudinous.

Stories about movie stars' romances are legion, but only a handful are true.

minister to attend to (MIN-iss-tur)

Use it as a verb rather than a noun, and it becomes much more ecumenical.

During the Civil War, the nurse Clara Barton ministered to many of the wounded soldiers and was known as the Angel of the Battlefield.

pedestrian boring (puh-DESS-tree-un)

So dull as to be duh. *Pedestrian* more commonly, of course, means someone who gets there on foot. Not the fastest or quickest way, is it? Rather plodding, in fact. From slow and plodding, it's just a few steps to prosaic, unimaginative, and oh-so-very ordinary.

Mass-market taste is often pedestrian, avoiding the racy and unusual.

purchase leverage (PUR-chiss)

You don't just buy stuff with *purchase*; you also buy influence, in the sense of securing an advantage.

Once his mentor resigned, he could get no purchase on the matter of a raise.

subscribe to agree with (sub-SKRĪB)

If you subscribe to the idea that words have more than one meaning, you'll know there's more to this word than the magazine subscription. *Subscribe* also means "to support, sanction, or agree with." Literally, *subscribe* is "to write." Not so literally, it's to put your stamp on something—that is, to support it.

Most Americans would subscribe to the idea that we live in a consumerist society; few would disagree.

tattoo a rhythmic drumming (ta-TOO)

Many a story we've heard about the other kind of tattoo being the result of barroom bravery occasioned by one too many beers. Curiously enough, *tattoo* as a drumbeat has its origins in the Dutch term for "closing time at the tavern."

He could feel his heart beating a stronger and stronger tattoo the closer he got to the tattoo parlor and its needle.

Bibliography

Print Resources

The American Heritage College Dictionary. 3rd ed. Edited by Robert B. Costello. Boston: Houghton Mifflin, 1993.

The American Heritage Dictionary. 4th ed. Edited by Joseph P. Pickett. New York: Bantam Dell, 2004.

Bragg, Melvyn. *The Adventure of English: The Biography of a Language.* London: Hodder and Stoughton, 2003.

Burgess, Gelett. *Burgess Unabridged: A Classic Dictionary of Words You Have Always Needed.* New York: Walker & Company, 2007.

Ehrlich, Eugene. *Amo, Amas, Amat and More: How to Use Latin to Your Own Advantage and to the Astonishment of Others.* New York: Harper & Row, 1987.

Espy, Willard R. *The Best of an Almanac of Words at Play.* Springfield, MA: Merriam-Webster, 1999.

Gooden, Philip. *Faux Pas? A No-Nonsense Guide to Words and Phrases from Other Languages.* New York: Walker & Company, 2005.

Gordon, James D. *The English Language: An Historical Introduction.* New York: Thomas Y. Crowell, 1972.

Kilpatrick, James J. *Fine Print: Reflections on the Writing Art.* Kansas City, MO: Andrews and McMeel, 1993.

Lederer, Richard. *Puns Spooken Here: Word Play for Halloween.* Charleston, SC: Wyrick & Company, 2006.

Liberman, Mark, and Geoffrey K. Pullum. *Far from the Madding Gerund and Other Dispatches from Language Log.* Wilsonville, OR: William, James & Co., 2006.

Lynch, Jack, ed. *Samuel Johnson's Dictionary: Selections from the 1755 Work That Defined the English Language.* Delray Beach, FL: Levenger Press, 2002.

————. *Samuel Johnson's Insults: A Compendium of Snubs, Sneers, Slights, and Effronteries from the Eighteenth-Century Master.* Delray Beach, FL, and New York: Levenger Press and Walker & Company, 2004.

Manser, Martin H. *The Facts on File Dictionary of Foreign Words and Phrases.* New York: Checkmark Books, 2002.

Merriam-Webster's Encyclopedia of Literature. Springfield, MA: Merriam-Webster, 1995.

Morris, William. *Your Heritage of Words: How to Increase Your Vocabulary Instantly.* New York: Dell, 1970.

The Oxford Dictionary of Allusions. Edited by Andrew Delahunty, Sheila Dignen, and Penny Stock. Oxford: Oxford University Press, 2001.

The Oxford English Dictionary. 2nd ed. Prepared by J. A. Simpson and E. S. C. Weiner. Oxford: Oxford University Press, 2004.

Plotnik, Arthur. *Spunk and Bite: A Writer's Guide to Punchier, More Engaging Language and Style.* New York: Random House, 2005.

The Random House Dictionary of the English Language. College ed. Edited by Laurence Urdang. New York: Random House, 1968.

Rattray, David, ed. *Success with Words: A Guide to the American Language.* Pleasantville, NY: Reader's Digest Association, 1983.

Shipley, Joseph T. *Dictionary of Word Origins.* Totowa, NJ: Littlefield, Adams, 1974.

Sommer, Elyse, with Dorrie Weiss. *Metaphors Dictionary*. Canton, MI: Visible Ink Press, 2001.

Trench, Richard Chenevix. *A Select Glossary of English Words Used Formerly in Senses Different from Their Present*. New York: Redfield, 1859.

Webster's College Dictionary. Edited by Robert B. Costello. New York: Random House, 1991.

Webster's Collegiate Dictionary. 5th ed. Springfield, MA: G. & C. Merriam, 1940.

Webster's New World Dictionary. 4th ed. Edited by Michael Agnes. New York: Pocket Books, 2003.

Westley, Miles. *The Bibliophile's Dictionary*. Cincinnati: Writer's Digest Books, 2005.

White, E. B. *Notes on Our Times*. Delray Beach, FL: Levenger Press, 2007.

Online Resources

American Heritage Dictionary of the English Language. 4th ed. Houghton Mifflin, 2006. http://dictionary.reference.com

AskOxford: www.askoxford.com

Encarta World English Dictionary. North American ed. Microsoft, 2007. http://encarta.msn.com

Encyclopaedia Britannica Online. Encyclopaedia Britannica, 2007. www.britannica.com

Merriam-Webster's Dictionary of Law. Merriam-Webster, 1996. http://dictionary.reference.com

OneLook: www.onelook.com

Online Etymology Dictionary: http://etymonline
.com

Random House Unabridged Dictionary. Random
House, 2006. http://dictionary.reference.com

Wikipedia: http://en.wikipedia.org

WordNet 3.0. Princeton University. http://
dictionary.reference.com

WordReference: www.wordreference.com

Acknowledgments

George Gibson made it possible for me to write this book, and that is just one of many reasons why I am indebted to him. Alison Fargis and Ellen Scordato took a chance and gave it to me—how can I ever thank you? To know that Meg Leder was such an enthusiastic and engaged editor is all (and everything) a writer needs.

Bob Greenman, Luise Erdmann, Katie Feiereisel, and Jennifer Eck provided invaluable fine-tuning. Thanks also to Thomas Chouvenc, Hallie Leighton, and Sachiko Hirata for their help with some finer points.

Encouragement is not a word in this book, but if it were, the definition would read: John Armato, Carmen Ayala, Karen and Luke Granger, Erik Moses, Dee Moustakas, Tina St. Pierre, and Ann Wylie.

Thanks to my gracious New York innkeeper, Tony Magner. As for patience, it's spelled h-u-s-b-a-n-d. Thank you, Nigel.

Index

Index

Index

Index

About the Author

Mim Harrison has been eavesdropping on English ever since her student days at Allegheny College. A year spent in England, often not understanding a word the English said, brought home to her the power of the language to both enlighten and befuddle. She was hooked.

She is a longtime professional writer and is also the founding editor of Levenger Press. Her first book, *Words at Work*, was published in 2007.

She hosts a website (www.mimharrison.com) and a blog, "Mim's the Word," at http://mimharrison.blogspot.com, where she invites other language lovers to have words with her.